PROJECT LEADER TO PROJECT BELIEVER

PROJECT LEADER TO PROJECT BELIEVER

John Kackley

2015

First Printing: 2015

ISBN 978-1-329-09538-0

CONTENTS

Foreword

I can't claim that the concept of project leadership, as distinct from project management, is entirely original with me. I do think I can bring a particular new slant to it, however. I wasn't just trying to make a subtle distinction (Really, Really Professional Project Managers, instead of just Project Management Professionals), but to make a complete distinction between the activities.

I started out with a few slides on project leadership, trying to shape the idea. Then several bolts of lightning hit me from different directions, and this book was born. From my war stories, it may seem like I've had more than my fair share of crazy, troubled projects. Actually, I suspect my track record is representative of project work generally speaking, and if there's anything notable here, it's the extent to which I analyze and review the experiences.

This represents nearly thirty years of work experience and reflection, and I hope you can learn from my experience and save yourself a few of those years!

Numerous people have helped me shape the ideas in this book as well as the written product. For the latter, I'd like to specifically thank Kevin Sheppard, Liz Miller, and Jennifer Hill for their support and feedback.

John Kackley, 2015

Introduction

Chapter 1: Project Leadership vs. Project Management

Chapter Summary

Project management is about project completion; project leadership is about project success.

Project Nag or Project Leader

Project management is big business. Every day, there are thousands of companies around the world trying to get things done. When they want to do something differently, they create a project to do it. And once they have a project, they need to manage it.

The Project Management Institute is just one of the many authorities advising would-be project managers on what to do and how to do it. You could fill a library and a good part of a warehouse with guides, manuals, and methodologies for project management.

Virtually all of them will tell you that a project needs to have a project charter, a project schedule, an issue log, a risk log, a project governance structure, and so on and so forth. Furthermore, there's metadata about the project. What methodology is it using? What tool will be used for documenting the project schedule? How will progress be tracked and reported?

Driving all of these tasks - managing them, if you will - is the job of the project manager.

What is commonly not the job of the project manager? Surprisingly to some - but not to others - the project manager is often not responsible for the actual delivery of the project objectives.

In many organizations, the project manager is an administrator. Better ones will be proactive and vocal, asking for status on deliverables before the day they're due, discussing issues before they've turned into burning oil platforms. But, as I often call them, they are professional nags. Everyone else is busy actually getting something done, and they're making sure their PowerPoint slides look good for the Steering Committee.

No wonder that in some organizations, project managers get very little respect.

And no wonder that in many organizations, they also get very little accomplished.

I worked with someone whose project management mantra was "Projects get behind a minute at a time, a day at a time." His point was that a project manager has to be on top of things every single moment, because once you've let something slip, the time's gone. You'll never get back the half a day that you lost because someone's computer went down or a key business contact was out sick.

I'll concede that there's a basic point there. You almost never make up time on a project. If you're late getting to your first milestone, you can safely push them all back.

I found this mantra tremendously annoying, however. First, it demanded an intensified experience as a project nag. Simply thinking in terms of human communication, there's a limit to how often and how rigorously you can ask people to provide updates on what they're doing. Ask enough times, you can be sure you're going to get evasions, estimates, and outright lies. Anything to get rid of you.

Second of all, it oversimplifies why projects are late, and suggests that every problem is either avoidable with proper foresight or fixable within its original timeframe.

Project management is about planning, predictions, and mitigations. I may sound critical of it, but there is no question that sound project management is key to project success.

Project leadership, on the other hand, is about owning the outcome and working with everyone involved to deliver it.

A project can be well run, knock off all its project management artifacts, produce its deliverables, come in on time and under budget, and still be a failure. That's what happens - best case scenario - when there is no leadership.

Here are some more specific ways in which a project leader differs from a project manager:

*   A project manager accepts resources as provided. A project leader constantly reviews project resources needed for project success.

*   A project manager accepts the project structure provided. A project leader constantly reviews the project structure for project success.

*   A project manager drives administrative completion of standard project management tasks. A project leader selects standard project management tasks as tools to enable delivery success.

*   A project manager focuses on project management deliverables. A project leader focuses on the delivery of the business outcome, regardless of the source of issues or solutions.

*   A project manager supports team delivery of a business
        outcome. A project leader collaborates on achievement
        of a business outcome.

In short, a project leader:

•   Is engaged with the team

•   Is engaged with the project sponsor and shares
        ownership of project outcomes

•   Takes personal responsibility for project success

This book is about what this means in detail, in day-to-day
situations, and how your actions in leadership translate into
project success.

Who's Ready to be a Project Leader?

As I mentioned before, there is a multitude of projects going on right now in every business, in every country in the world. They can be fit into categories in various ways. You can sort them by size - by the number of people on the project, by their budget, or by project duration. You can organize them by the nature of the deliverable - a new computer system, a process, a document, or a new organization. Or you can filter them by the nature of the problem being solved - such as fixing an old problem or trying something new.

Another dimension not usually used for categorization has to do with the source of the people on the project. I happen to be a consultant, and I am virtually always engaged in a project model. There's a budget, an objective, a beginning and an end. In most (but not all) cases, I'm 100% assigned to the project, and so are most of my teammates.

Plenty of projects don't look like that at all. A team - say, a procurement department - decides it needs to design a new form to handle a type of procurement that they haven't done before. It's a small activity, in the grand scheme of things. There are no consultants, no external stakeholders. There may not even really be a budget. The members of the team are everyone in the department, they work on it when they get the chance, and it will be done when everyone's happy with the result.

And the project manager? That might just be one member of the team. Someone remembers that they should have a project charter, and the supervisor suggests a status report would be nice and maybe they should keep track of how much time everyone's spending on this. Hey, presto change-o, you've got a project, you've got some project management artifacts, and now you've got a project manager, too.

Does this project manager need to think about project leadership? Does this project manager even need to think about Project Management Professional certification?

In my book, the answer's definitely "no" for the second question, but how about the first?

If the project manager is just a member of the department, they're going to be pretty engaged in the work anyway. They may not take on a "leader" role, but they'll be just as engaged as any other team member. Maybe that's not really project leadership.

What if someone assigns a project manager from outside the group, just to help keep things rolling? That project manager might be doing the same sort of thing for half a dozen different projects. No time for project leadership, and no demand for it, either.

But if nobody commits to the project, and is there to stir the rest of the team to action when the initial enthusiasm wears off, the project runs the risk of going softly to sleep, never to be seen or heard from again.

Project leadership is about how a person in a position of engagement leads a team to complete its objective.

Project leadership is about how you, as an individual team member working within a project framework, take responsibility for the project's success.

Not everyone who plays the role of project manager has to step up to be a project leader, and project leadership isn't limited to project managers. Project leadership is not about a title or an assignment.

However, the activity of project leadership most commonly connects with the role of the project manager, and as a consequence, this book is written to connect leadership to typical project management activities.

Your commitment as a project manager leads to leadership. Your leadership encourages a collective drive to the project goal. It converts your teammates into project *believers* - people who support and commit to the project objective.

Are you ready for project leadership?

The Mission

This mission of this book is to examine what it means to be a project leader, not just a project manager. We'll go through many aspects of projects and how leadership works in them.

Project leadership is a diverse activity: its components are not sequential, hierarchical, or necessarily parallel in scope, scale, or priority. To reflect this, I think of the building blocks of project leadership as skills in orbit around the focusing principle, as suggested in the diagram below.

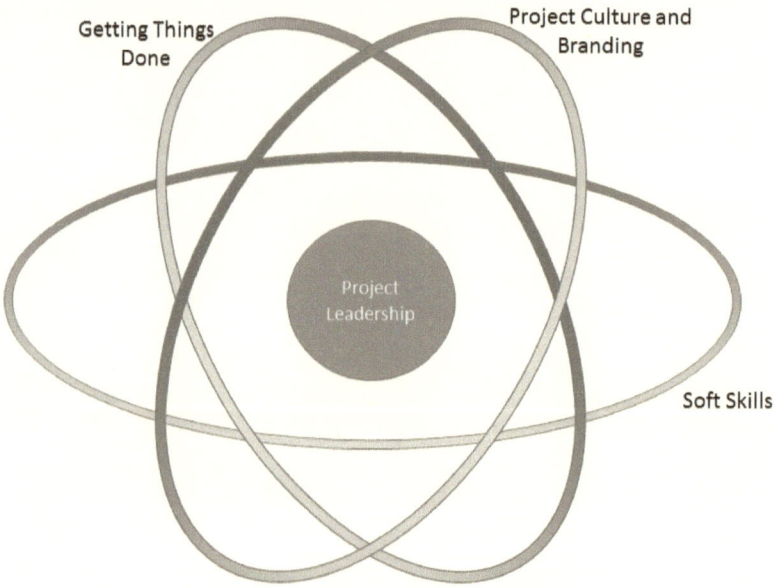

FIGURE 1. PROJECT LEADERSHIP'S ORBITING SKILLS.

We'll use these orbits to organize the content of this book.

In chapters 2 and 3, we'll discuss a project's culture and branding.

In chapters 4 through 8, we'll talk about some of the hands-on responsibilities of being a project leader getting things done on a project.

In chapters 9 through 11, we'll cover the "soft" skills of communication, mentorship, and personal development.

Then we'll wrap up everything in chapter 12 with a rousing song to get us off the stage. We'll recap the core of project leadership, and see how this leads us to the next stage, that of being a project believer.

The examples and lessons discussed are from things I've seen and absorbed in over 25 years of project work in various roles. I've worked with numerous clients in virtually every industry, on projects using many different technologies and driving to outcomes in many different business functions. The diversity of experience has been key to seeing how the pieces come together so I can share them here.

My father, somewhat a connoisseur of business self-help books, told me once that he usually hopes to get two new insights out of any book of that sort. I hope you'll find two of your own in here.

Chapter Wrap-up

Project leadership is about how you, as an individual team member working within a project framework, take responsibility for the project's success.

In short, a project leader:

- Is engaged with the team

- Is engaged with the project sponsor and shares ownership of project outcomes

- Takes personal responsibility for project success

Project Culture and Branding

Chapter 2: The Culture of Companies and Projects

Chapter Summary

Companies and projects have personalities; a project leader needs to understand them and account for them to enable project success.

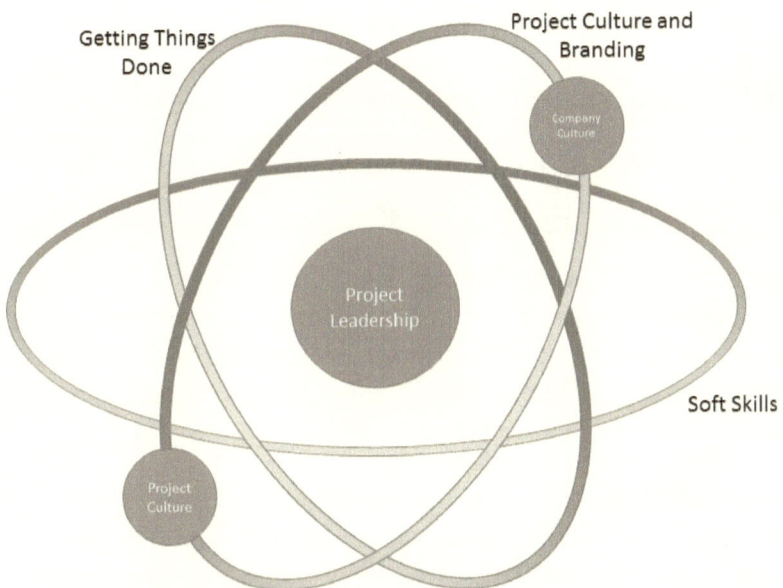

What Does the Organization Value?

Any project exists within a larger context. Ignoring the background cosmic radiation (like geopolitics and society), that context is the culture of the organization in which the project is created.

It has been trendy to discuss the culture of various companies, and sometimes this is taken too far. Social anthropologists, desperate to create relevance for their field, have taken to the business world, eager to study traditions, ceremonies, and hierarchies in an artificial community.

So let's not call it a corporate culture. Let's call it a personality.

Every organization has a personality, and it's part of being a project leader to understand it. A company's personality is just like a person's. If you don't understand it, you'll have all sorts of communication failures. For a project leader, this likely means the failure of your project.

For the most part, the values that drive people in an organization are the values they bring in from outside, and therefore conducting sociological analyses on them is a waste of effort.

However, companies do have their unique qualities which provide a context to their projects, and a wise project leader pays attention to these things.

The two primary aspects of company culture that matter day to day are:

1.   What does the company value?

2.   How do people interact in the organization?

In assessing what a company values, there are two sub-categories: what the company as a whole values, and what the individuals in the company value.

It will often be easier to see what the individuals value, with more time being needed to observe what the company values.

For example, some organizations, especially high-tech companies with highly visible leaders, develop a cult of personality. Steve Jobs, Bill Gates, and Mark Zuckerberg were all founders of massively successful high-tech companies. This often spawns of admiration and imitation, and sometimes not just within the organization itself. How many pretentious consultants have you seen going with the monochrome mock turtleneck look of Steve Jobs?

In Microsoft, many employees took on billg's style of flame emails, mistaking an immature executive's style of communication as an indication of decisiveness, hipness, and genius. I'd like to think Gates himself has matured in his communication; many of his former employees kept the old style of communication long after Gates himself had stepped out of the picture.

In most older companies, individuals will value what the company values. There's a collaborative process where the company's values are shaped by its employees, while the employees take on the values of the company. Also, when a person's values differ too drastically from the company's, the person is likely to seek opportunities elsewhere, leaving the more aligned employees in place.

An example: a company I've worked with recently has a culture that rewards tackling issues and getting them resolved. Typically ignored are planning things out ahead of time, and defining business processes and solution approaches. The firefighting is rewarded because it's visible and demonstrates commitment. Also, it avoids dealing with schedule and resource constraints.

On the other hand, what you get in an environment like that is a constant focus on the negative. Nobody ever wants to say things are satisfactory. Instead, everything is another problem to be solved, because there's a prize hidden under every solution.

The Mail Must Get Through

Another cultural example comes from FedEx. When I worked there I learned that they had gone through different phases, such as one where information technology was valued, for example. The dominant theme in my time there was successful delivery at any cost.

Remember the movie "Castaway" with Tom Hanks, and how his character is fixated on time and keeps himself sane by keeping a package safe until he can deliver it himself? FedEx didn't have a lot to do with the making of that movie, but those were certainly their values. I heard many times about how FedEx made a special flight to deliver medicine to a sick little girl. Regional managers had to have complete discretion in order to ensure that deliveries were made. Nobody wanted to be the guy who stopped medicine from getting to that sick little girl.

Those values came into play on my project. We were planning the implementation of a procurement system, but we were taking a holistic view of it: people, process, and technology all had to be aligned.

In the process area, we spent a lot of time assessing process best practices in procurement and how they could assist the client.

A significant case in point is spending limits: how much money could somebody spend before a manager or someone else had to approve it? I forget exactly what the spending limit was when we got there, but was on the order of thousands of dollars each, regardless of who the employee was. This meant that, any given time, the collective employees of FedEx could commit the company to hundreds of millions of dollars of expense with no approval by anyone. Naturally, we put together a standard signing limit table: the average employee could to spend up to $250 without approval, a supervisor could spent $1500 or so, and so on.

When we presented these ideas, however, we got no response. Eventually we were able to extract an explanation. If that spending limit meant a part couldn't get purchased to fix the truck to make a delivery on time, it wouldn't be acceptable. No one was willing to take any part of that risk.

The technical side of the equation was equally frustrating. Part of the planned system implementation was an ERP called PeopleSoft, which was especially noted at the time for its vast configurability. Any business rule, any business function, could be configured to suit the company's needs.

We explained this to our client, but kept getting the same confusing response. How does it work? they would ask. How does the system say it has to work?

You can configure it, we kept saying. How do you want it to work?

Eventually we figured out what was going on. Our team members weren't dumb. They were well aware that no limitations could be put into the business process that would conflict with the power of a regional manager. If the system could be configured, it could be configured with any parameters desired. They would have to go ask people what those parameters should be. The explanation would reveal the broad capabilities of configuration that were available, and then all hell would break loose. The loosest possible business rules would be demanded. Anything to provide ultimate flexibility when a package needed to be delivered.

To solve that, our team wanted to tell everyone that it wasn't configurable at all. They wanted the system to dictate all the process best practices we were discussing, so they would never have to deal with the demands for flexibility, which they knew would ultimately undermine the whole project.

How Many Trucks Can I Buy For That?

Quite in contrast to FedEx was a truck leasing company in Iowa. They were quite possibly the most miserly company I've ever worked with, and they took great pride in that assessment.

The company was family-owned: the founder was still the chairman of the board, and his grandson was the president. Besides owning this company (and the high-rise office building it partially occupied), they owned the local convention hotel and other assets.

An example of the comprehensiveness of their frugality: they controlled an airport rental car franchise, one of the taxi companies, and a used car lot. A car would start its life as a rental car and eventually transition into being a taxi. When it got too old for that, they'd sell it at their lot.

Some of the cars became company cars. Every manager was given a company car. That might seem grand, except remember that all of these cars started life as rental cars. Also, the company had operations throughout the Midwest, but mostly not anywhere convenient to air travel. The managers were expected to drive wherever they were going. Driving to the corners of Iowa were one thing, but it never sounded like fun when they had to drive from Des Moines to Indianapolis.

They made a vertical industry out of being cheap.

If all of that didn't make the convincing case that this was a cheap company, in contrast to FedEx's looseness on spending limits, this company had a very strict one: any expense of $250 or more - *any* expense - had to be approved by the president of the company.

There was a business justification to it that played a role in working with this company. As a truck leasing company, they knew to several decimal points of accuracy just how much revenue they could earn from spending $100,000 on a truck. If you came to them and said, "Here's a million dollar project you need to do," you had to be darned sure that you could make more money for them than ten new trucks would.

We started out with an assessment of their information technology department. We calculated the percentage of their revenue that went to research and development in this area, and compared that to the standard for their industry. As I recall, 1.5% was the standard, and they were at 0.9%. Their reaction was, "Woo-hoo! Look how efficient we are!"

It was a real challenge to make the case to them that lower wasn't necessarily better. In an information-driven industry, you need to keep making investments so you don't fall behind. You really have to be on your game, with a completely solid case, when every time you propose an expense you hear:

"How many trucks can I buy for that?"

Culture From the Bottom Up

While employees usually take on the direction and values of the company, sometimes it works in reverse and from the bottom up.

Some years ago I was proposed for a project at a client. My first interview was with a resource manager. Her job was to prepare me for the interview with the project sponsors, and it was one of the strangest interviews I've ever been in. It's common to learn in an interview what's important to the project or the company - some insight into whether you'll be a good fit. I heard that in spades in this interview.

"An organization is informed by the people who work there," I was told. "Most of our employees are female in their late twenties, and their style of communication and teamwork is the standard in the company."

The resource manager went on to explain that meetings are never used for problem resolution. No one will say anything when the meeting is structured that way. What you do, she said, is to arrive at the solution outside of the meeting, and then meet individually with the attendees beforehand. Then everyone can join in and agree with the solution that you present.

I must say I found the openness refreshing, even if the stereotyping was a bit painful.

Since I prefer to work collaboratively, including using working sessions to arrive at solutions, I expect this would have been a gruesome experience for me. I was not a bit disappointed to learn than they'd selected another consultant for the role: I can just imagine the challenges I would have faced in trying to lead a project in that culture.

Project Personalities

Projects have personalities, too.

Being made up of smaller numbers of individuals, they can be more reflective of the idiosyncrasies of their members. If that personality is bought into by most of the members, it can make the team a very tight-knit group.

While company personalities can drive from official mission statements and the like, project personalities are less formal and more unpredictable. They are also typically more narrowly focused, just as a project is focused on a single objective.

They usually derive from one of three sources:

1.   Attributes or traits (such as past experience or sense of humor) shared by a number of the team members

2.   The values and personality of a key member of the project, such as the project sponsor or project manager

3.   The history of the project

The common thread here is that you don't get to pick the project personality. You may not really see what the project personality is until the project's nearly complete. And you certainly can't predict it.

A project's personality can manifest as a certain gallows humor, perhaps if the project has had numerous setbacks. An "us against the world" theme has been the tone for many projects.

It may show up as a commitment to heroic efforts to deliver on promises.

A project team might develop a personality around the work styles and behavior of its members, such as uncommon working hours or the use of communications tools unknown to others in the organization.

Most of these things may seem more like quirks than personalities. They may seem insignificant or harmless compared to the company personalities.

Nevertheless, a project leader still needs to understand his project's personality. First of all, the personality may actually be detrimental to project success, such as in the case when it is extremely negative or overly confrontational.

A greater risk comes when the personalities of the host company and the project clash. In the FedEx example above, the project team's desire for innovation and improvement was warped by the need to fit inside the company's laser focus on facilitating deliveries. That project was eventually scaled down to a minor technical improvement of an existing process.

Another challenge comes from the nature of projects. A project has a plan and a goal, and typically is disbanded once the goal has been reached. For some projects, such as software implementations, the project team and its activities may be subsumed into the permanent organization.

While this usually has other impacts, such as a reduction in cost, this also serves to remove the project team's goals and personality from the equation.

In another example in my experience, a large project team consisting of independent contractors was responsible for delivering a major software product. The team established its own processes and personality, using tools, methodology, and work practices that were unfamiliar to the company. It was challenging to transfer even part of the project team's activities to the permanent IT organization. The transition was rough and the outcomes frequently unsatisfactory. Also, attempts to have teams addressing parallel work suffered similar difficulties, as they just couldn't work with the larger project team.

Managing the Personalities

As a project leader, you have to manage the company and project personalities as much as the personalities of any team member or stakeholder. Naturally, managing the personalities begins with recognizing them.

Try asking some of these questions about the organization or project:

*   What are the stories that people in the organization tell about its past? What are the company's founding myths?

*   When people talk about other employees and their performance, what characteristics do they speak positively about? What do they speak negatively about?

*   When somebody says that something can't be done, what reasons do they give? Do you hear the same reasons over and over?

*   What behavior or speech do you see that's out of the ordinary?

*   When things go wrong, what do people talk about? Blame? Fixing the problem? Explaining the source of the mistake?

*   When things go well, what do people talk about? Pride in the organization? Heroic efforts? A star performer?

*   What does the organization's structure tell you about it?

*   What tools do people use to communicate with each other? Do leaders welcome direct contact or force employees through a gate keeper?

*   What are the common threads to the stories of people
        who have been with the organization a long time?

In all likelihood, you won't be able to get very deep on a lot of
these questions with limited exposure. Some of these things
take time, and you may revise your interpretation several
times before settling on a description of the company's core.

Over time, however, you should be able to identify a number of
points which describe the organization's personality. Having
done so, you should treat these points the same way as any
other project risks, documenting them and planning a
mitigation strategy.

You should do this even when the item seems benign or even
positive. Few personality attributes of an organization are
purely "good" or "bad", and any of them can have an impact on
your project. These bullets may tell you how a company will
make decisions or respond to challenges, and the very least
should tell you the sort of questions they will ask.

Let's look at an example of this that shows how tricky it can be
to deal with company personalities.

At another client of mine, the project's objective was (in my
words) attempting to make Microsoft SharePoint work like
Facebook. I thought I was doing a great job to question this
immediately, as it sounded like a really bad idea. Why do this?
I asked. Why not call up Facebook and try to buy a private
instance?

I was told that the client had a strong bias towards building
things themselves, so I should simply drop the question. So we
built a prototype that tried to twist SharePoint into
uncomfortable shapes, and given that it was the sort of project
that should never have been attempted, I think we did a pretty

good job. The client? The client was ultimately dissatisfied and proceeded to look for a product to buy.

So what happened? We thought we understood the company's personality, and maybe we were right. In the end, though, they did exactly what we thought they wouldn't do. What could we have done differently?

I think there are several factors at play here.

First, we may have simply been wrong about the company's personality. That assessment was handed to me by someone else on my second day with the company, and I had no information to make that assessment myself.

Second, right or wrong about their personality, I shouldn't have let myself be warned off when I asked the question initially. I should have taken that up with the project stakeholders to hear their thoughts on it.

Third, it's always possible that the only way the company was going to realize the need to purchase a solution was to see how difficult it was to build something custom. From that perspective, our prototype was valuable: we helped them get to a conclusion they could not have reached on their own.

In short, having been alerted to the company's personality, I should have confronted it and talked about it. Leaving it unspoken simply led to frustration.

It's to avoid that frustration that a project leader learns to work within the personality of his environment.

Chapter Wrap-up

Companies and projects have personalities, and as a project leader, you have to work within them to achieve success.

You should consciously identify the key points of your company's and project's personalities. These elements of your environment should be considered among your project's risk factors.

You can influence your project's personality, but much of it will develop naturally from your team's internal operations.

Chapter 3: Personal and Project Branding
Chapter Summary
Use personal branding to define yourself as a project leader, and use project branding to define your project's identity.

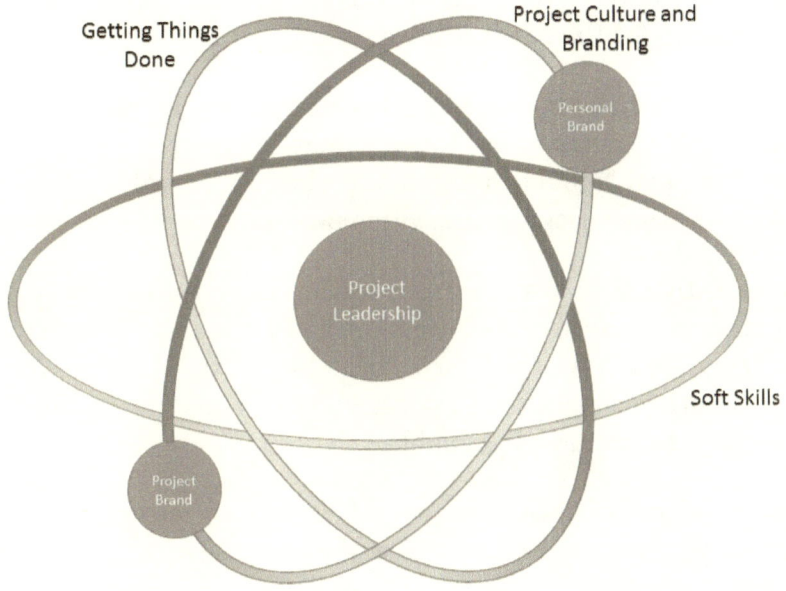

Earning Brand Recognition

The concept of a brand came from people burning some kind of identifying mark on their product, whether it was a barrel, a pot, or a steer. Sometimes the brand was useful simply in sorting things out, but from an early date (and we're talking literally thousands of years ago) it was being used to claim a differentiation for the product it was stamped on.

We have various terms related to this that go beyond the esoteric world of marketing. "Brand name", "brand recognition", and "famous makers" all relate to the value of the brand itself being recognized as valuable.

The idea is that people will attach value to the brand. They'll buy a product because of its brand, or they'll pay more because of the brand. We have the idea of "brand loyalty", where people will stick with a certain brand, even when trying a new product or a cheaper substitute is available.

The development of brands was significant in American business history because it was part of nationalizing the economy. Establishing a national brand included convincing consumers that locally-produced alternatives weren't better, and that association (through consumption) of a nationally branded product represented a progressive, modern viewpoint.

Branding enabled the sale not just of the assumed quality and value of a product based on its name, but the sale of intangibles to go along with the product. What brand you selected served to identify you with a subset of society. You're a different kind of hip and trendy depending on the brand of clothes you buy or the beer you drink. Ownership of a certain kind of car associates one with certain (presumably positive and admirable) attributes. That reflected aura became part of the price tag.

That last item - the values associated to a car brand - particularly highlights what a brand has come to mean. A brand reflects values. A certain hotel brand might mean "opulent luxury for business travelers", while another means "cheap, clean, and relatively safe place for truckers to stay". A retailer's brand might mean "one place to shop and save", while another might mean "highest quality clothes", and a third might suggest "clever items to buy for Father's Day when you can't think of anything else".

Now, these different unofficial labels might not really be what the brands' owners intend, at least not in as many words. Yet they might still be the way the brand is seen: the brand may have escaped the control of its owner.

Branding is reputation: you can do your best to establish it, but you can't control it.

Your task as a project leader is to identify your personal brand and that of your project, and then protect its meaning.

The Value of a Personal Brand

While corporate brands have continued to evolve, and may in some ways have declined in value, the concept of a personal brand has developed.

The idea of a personal brand is not so you can sell yourself like a can of baked beans. The idea is to establish an identity for yourself, and then to reinforce this identity with your communication and work. To some extent, this is intertwined with your online presence in social media or blogging.

Personal branding is often connected closely to people who work as independent contractors or who are starting their own company. In this case, the personal brand looks very much like a corporate brand, and with similar consequences.

For example, in 1981, Cadillac produced the Cimarron. This looked a great deal like a Chevy Cavalier, and was built in the same manufacturing facility. This was perceived as damaging the Cadillac brand, which stood for quality and a certain exclusiveness.

Similarly, a person who is starting their own business may be tempted to take on work or charge rates that are not in keeping with the brand they hope to establish. Having done this just to get going, they may then find that they've set a market expectation for the type of work they do or the rates they charge.

Personal branding can be a factor in your perception in an overall corporate setting. Some years ago I transferred with a consulting company from one office to another. I remained on the same project, which was working on a methodology tool for implementing a packaged software product, and spent another year and a half working remotely on the same project. Without more exposure and communication, people were often unaware of my other skills and experience.

Personal branding is establishing your identity among the people you work with (or hope to work with). It describes your skills, your values, and the type of work you thrive on.

Done well, establishing a brand for yourself is an entirely positive thing. It helps people connect with you with certain work. Not only will people realize that you are experienced with a certain skill, technology, or business process, they may perceive you as an expert and the "go to guy" for that work. It helps people shape their perception of you in absence of other information, and gives them a more proactive impression of you. You're not just "the guy who can do stuff", you're "the guy who does X, Y, and Z".

If you're in the position of being able to turn down work, it conveniently helps screen out the kinds of work that you don't want to do.

Of particular interest to the context of project leadership, personal branding can be used to make that clear as well. You can make it clear through your brand that you add value through leadership and ownership, and that you are not simply skilled in administrative project management.

With this, you not only set the expectation from the beginning, but you can help to shape the values of the client or boss you want to work with. They might think they needed a project manager; by changing the vocabulary of the discussion, you have opened it up to them that they need a project leader. You have also opened up further areas for discussion about how the project should be run and what its values should be.

Building a Personal Brand

There are numerous books devoted to how one builds one's personal brand. I'll summarize the key points from most of them here.

*   Define your professional identity.

*   Breathe life into your brand (saying it makes it so).

*   Live it.

In the next few sections, we'll go through these steps.

Defining a Professional Identity

The first step is one of the trickiest for a lot of people. Who *are* you? What do you want to be known for?

Many people get stuck trying to write a resume with an objective section at the beginning. "I'm applying to your job opening," they think. "Obviously that's a job I want. Why should I have to write an objective?"

As a result, many people never write that section of their resume. While people seem to survive this, the real point to the exercise is *not* how to write an objective on a resume. The point is that you should know what you want and how you want to do it.

I wouldn't expect everyone to want to broadcast that at any given point in time. Sometimes you just need a job. Sometimes you *need* a job so badly that you don't bother thinking about what you *want*.

However, if you can't define for yourself what you want, you'll never be able to tell anyone else. If you want people to value your unique contributions, to advocate for you, or to ask for your assistance directly, you need to be able to tell them your story.

So what should a statement of personal identity look like?

Many writers will discuss writing your own mission statement, and maybe this is very similar. I'd like think of it as being a little more malleable than that, however. Imagine you've got one paragraph of a cover letter, one paragraph on a social website profile, or fifteen seconds of a job interview to tell someone who you really are.

What would you say?

You can certainly produce a mission statement in the classic, labored, run-on sentence mode. You can also say something off-beat and memorable, but I don't think you want to lead with "I like cheese".

I'd also try to avoid being too metaphorical.

I think there was a fad some years ago, probably descending from Barbara Walters' interview questions on the order of, "What kind of a tree would you be?" I remember doing campus interviews some years back and all of the interviews were done in a hotel ballroom with no dividers. When you were in the middle of your own interview, you could focus and not notice anything around you, but when you were done and writing up your notes, you could pick up the thread of nearby interviews.

I heard the young lady at the next table ask my colleague, "If Accenture was a car, what kind of a car would it be?"

I believe the answer given was that Accenture would be some kind of luxury sports car, agile but powerful. Maybe you could work with that sort of answer for your professional definition.

Of course, people I've told this story to often suggest that the correct answer was "Accenture is like a truck. It gets where it needs to go and runs you over if you get in the way." That just tells you the risks in trying to control the message.

Personally, I'd recommend assembling a definition that indicates not the skills you have, but the outcome or organization you like being a part of. Some way of communicating the passion you have for it works, too. It's tough, but I'd try to avoid using clichés. They make it sound like you copied your professional statement or career objective out of a book.

One last note on this. People look at objective statements on resumes in a couple of different ways. Some rewrite the statement for every job they are applying for. It might be suitable to craft the statement to fit a job, but your professional statement for your personal brand should be a more definite statement, not something that changes to fit the circumstance.

Another common response to objective statements is that, by being clear and precise about what your objective is and what kind of what you want do, you will seem less flexible. "If I say this," goes the reasoning. "People will think I'll be difficult to work with."

There's certainly a fine line between resolute and stubborn. Your statement and your behavior have to come together to show that you're on the positive side of that line.

Breathing Life into Your Brand

Having set down your objective, mission statement, or professional identity, it's now time to make it come to life.

The first thing to do is tell people about it. This is no time to be shy. People won't know that you're John Doe, project troubleshooter extraordinaire, or Jane Smith, graphic design wizard, if you don't say so yourself.

It's not that you should inflate your credentials or invent awards.

What you should be doing is highlighting the experiences that you want people to associate with you.

In person, you can tell people you work with about yourself. It doesn't have to be a formal presentation; it can simply be references to your points of view. It can even just be a matter of showing your enthusiasm for the activities you enjoy most.

Imagine what you would conclude if someone on your team said, "I just love working on test automation! I really get into it!" After you concluded that they weren't being sarcastic, you'd have to conclude that they really enjoyed test automation. As a project leader, you'd look forward to opportunities to leverage that enthusiasm.

Another primary vehicle for spreading your personal brand nowadays is social media. Tools like Facebook, LinkedIn, blogs, technical discussion forums, and Twitter are all part of establishing that brand identity. This comes in two parts: who you say you are, and what you show you can do.

To establish your identity, you can write your profile on these tools to indicate what you're interested in. That personal statement you just did - that goes here.

You can post content that demonstrates your interest (as well as your accomplishments). Contribute to discussions to demonstrate insight and experience. Answer questions. Engage in discussions (even if you don't have a really solid answer). You can also use sites like SlideShare to show your visually-oriented portfolio.

Remember the old "New Yorker" cartoon of the dog using a computer to post content on the internet, and he says, "On the internet, no one knows I'm a dog"? One of the dreams of the internet economy is that you can be judged by your contributions and insight as seen on the internet. Your college, your title, your age - none of them are important in that world.

An underlying idea of personal branding is that people will take you at your own valuation of yourself. It works the same way as going to work dressed one way if you want to present yourself as the hip, creative type, and another way if you want to be serious and professional. People see the image you present, and most of the time, they don't have the time or information to think anything else. You make it easy for them by telling them what to expect from you. You're going to have to back up your claims at some point, but you can get the conversation started on your terms.

Remember that you're not trying to recap your resume in every venue. Your brand should be an extension that goes beyond your resume in promoting yourself, *showing* (not telling) who you are and what you can do.

You can get pretty creative here, and subtlety is okay. In the case of one project manager I worked with, he wore a suit even though the dress code was business casual. "I wanted my clients to know that there's nothing casual about how I treated their business," he explained to me. Wearing a suit was part of his personal brand.

You should still keep some reasonable limits in mind, however. Unlike corporate brands, you'll probably want to stop short of having your own jingle or mascot. I knew an executive assistant at Exxon Mobil who had started collecting stuffed toy tigers (the Exxon mascot) and had an entire office full of orange and black striped critters. Cute and memorable, but it didn't necessarily add anything to her personal brand. While it did suggest that she was likable (most of the tigers were presents from people who worked with her), it did also send a message that she worked in a cluttered workspace.

A lot of the concept of personal branding may be around making yourself more successful. Promoting yourself and your brand are associated with being better known; being better known is equated with greater success. I'd like to propose that it's possible that your branded identity isn't going to make more money or be better known than your commoditized, conformist self. Think of it more as self-realization - sharing your personal brand can help make you more successful at being who you want to be.

Living Your Brand as a Project Leader

The ideas discussed here are meaningful regardless of the brand you're trying to establish. You've defined who you are and who you want to be, and you've started to communicate this message. This is all a waste if you don't live the message.

Let's bring it back to defining yourself as a project leader.

It's valuable to establish and refresh your brand. You want to maintain a reputation, and you want to project yourself as the sort of person people want to go to for certain work.

Specifically in our context, however, is the value of making the distinction between project leadership and project management.

Your resume may say "project manager" on it. You might have a certification for it. The roles you've played on past projects may scream "project manager" no matter how you may have tried to disguise it. When you get introduced as a candidate for a role, you're probably introduced as a project manager.

All the way along, you've let the environment define who you are.

Part of being a project leader is not just doing the work differently, but setting the expectation that your client or boss is getting something different when they bring you on board. Your brand helps start the conversation about project leadership and the distinguishing value that you bring as that kind of leader.

The starting point for this is the discussion that kicks off your connection to the project. Once you've absorbed the details of the situation and your role, you can start playing it back from a project leader perspective. What can you own? What will you have responsibility for?

It continues throughout your connection with the project, as you demonstrate leadership at every stage. You live your brand by focusing on the delivery of success, not just the completion of a work plan.

Also, don't forget that as you live your brand, your brand has a life of its own. Keep building the brand by sharing your accomplishments and portfolio. Answer questions, engage in discussions, and mentor others to help maintain and broaden your brand, not just in-person, but on the web as well.

How Does Personal Branding Translate into Project Branding?

Personal branding has entire books written about it. Project branding does not, at least not how we're going to talk about it here.

Projects have reputations, too - or, if you like, they have brands. Think about your past projects. How many were the "death march project", the "strategy project", or the "save the business project"?

Projects build reputations within their companies. Too often the reputations are negative. They build a reputation for being unreliable, over budget, or having high employee turnover. You have to overcome that reputation every day.

Sometime project reputations escape into the wild and become known beyond company walls, especially in technical areas. Microsoft's Project Longhorn (which eventually produced the Microsoft Windows Vista operating system) is an example of this, with consequences to the product's reputation and Microsoft's share price.

Why care about project branding? Besides the Longhorn example, even in an internal situation it can impact funding or issue resolution. When you have earned a good reputation, the entire project will be trusted more to make good use of funding, for example.

Anyhow, everyone wants to look good. While you'll do a lot to shape your project's brand in your own image, your own brand will reflect the project's brand (along with its success).

What's more, a brand has some other impacts. A good brand can attract good people who want to be a part of it. A bad brand can drive people away, leading to them to leave the project or disengage, not committing fully to the project.

On most projects, nobody thinks about the project's reputation (its brand) until it's too late.

I was on a project once in Las Vegas. It had been turned into a bit of a death march, and people commonly asked to be removed from the project. By the way, it may sound cool to be on a project in Las Vegas, and that does have the advantage that you never have a hard time finding something to eat at weird hours of the day, but mostly it's like working anywhere else. Except, of course, for the gambling addiction problems (seriously: we had three people we had to remove from the project due to gambling problems).

Anyhow, it was not a happy situation. A project video meant to build team spirit included a reference to the movie "Goodfellas" wherein project leads discussed how to organize the shallow graves of project members in the desert. "Staff over here, consultants over here, managers over there." Seriously. It actually seemed reasonably funny at the time, but it doesn't take much to see it as completely humorless and indicative of serious problems.

Due to some organizational shifts, the project picked up new leadership. The work was reorganized, the budget redone, and the team morale revived. Soon people were asking to join the project. The brand had been completely rebuilt.

What if you make building the brand part of your job as project leader?

Don't manage a budget, manage an issue, or produce a deliverable just as an item to check off on the way to a completed work plan. Tackle it as a building block for the reputation you want to have.

Does the company culture tend to overestimate the risk of deployments? Over-prepare for the deployment to eliminate the risk, and become the project that manages deployments well.

Is the company used to projects which routinely exceed their budgets? Focus on developing a quality budget at one end of the process, or control project expenses and scope at the other end, to become the project that meets its budget.

This may make it sound as if a project brand is really just delivering high quality results, with certain added ingredients of reputation and spin. There's more, however. It's also:

*   Building a project brand that mirrors the commitment of your personal brand

*   Owning the vocabulary of the discussion

*   A reflection of where the project came from and where it's going

We'll talk about each of these in the following sections.

Personal Brand, Project Brand

As a project leader, you want your project team to share your values. You'd like your team members to do the work as you would, care as much about the deliverable as you do, and have the same commitment.

These things won't always be possible. You can't clone yourself and play every role on the project.

However, there are several foundational areas where you can set a positive tone for your team.

*   Teamwork

*   Quality

*   Attitude

*   Communication

*   Respect for others

We'll talk about each of these briefly here.

Teamwork is team members taking appropriate ownership of tasks or objectives, following through on commitments, cooperating with each other for mutual support, and having a shared belief in the project objective.

Quality as a habit is about establishing an expectation of quality, along with standard, expected activities to ensure quality. Peer reviews of code, deliverables, or presentations can all help build quality as a habit.

Attitude is the tone and energy used in participating in the project. If you use a negative or defeatist tone, focusing on bad luck or bad circumstances, others around you will pick that up and echo it. If you use a positive tone, reinforcing it with praise and celebration of victories, people will pick that up instead.

Communication is the expectations of project communications. Can anyone speak to anyone on the project, or are there protected channels? Are there any topics off-limits? What respect is given to concerns that are voiced?

Respect for others is showing respect for the capabilities and contributions of everyone on the team. While it has a general meaning, in a project sense you can extend it to the view that everyone on the team plays a role, and everyone has something to offer for the project's success.

For most of these, you show leadership by setting the example with your behavior. In some cases, you may be able to drive behavior through project practices (such as quality reviews). Either way, your project team will take the cue on these values from you.

As a project leader, you have a specific challenge in this area. It's easy create a negative tone on your team through your own behavior. It's much harder to simply whistle a happy tune and have everyone join you. It takes work, reinforcement, and coaching. Your team has to see that it's genuine, not delusional, and contributes to project success. If any of those are missing, people will notice and your modeling of positive behavior will struggle to make a dent.

Owning the Vocabulary

Ever have that meeting where you're trying to make a point, and your audience just doesn't get it? They keep asking about things you don't want to talk about. Maybe they keep referring to events in the past. You've solved those old problems and put them behind you, but you just can't escape them. Or, you keep saying, "We completed deliverables X, Y, and Z, isn't that great" and your audience says, "What was the rate of defects?"

What's happened in each of those examples is that you've lost control of the vocabulary of the project.

The vocabulary is the words used to discuss the objective of the project, how the work is being done (i.e., methodology or work breakdown), and how success is defined.

To be cynical about it, the idea comes from classics on propaganda. When you get people to use your words to discuss the situation, you then get them to use your model of how to think. That association can seem negative, but it really just reflects human psychology. If a stakeholder or team member uses a different paradigm to view the project, they won't truly be a part of the team. As a result, every conversation will be a struggle, not just over facts or whether a status box should be "red" or "yellow", but over the basic way the world works.

To own the vocabulary, you have to set it at an early date, and then use it consistently. If you feel the objective of the project is a working prototype, not necessarily exposed to actual users, then you keep using that word and that explanation. If you shift to "proof of concept" or "limited pilot" - anything that has a different interpretation - a listener may think the scope now includes deployment to users. The scope didn't really change. It wasn't supposed to change. But the wrong words may have implied that there was a change.

The vocabulary can be especially critical in discussing how the work is being done and how progress is being measured. On an Agile project, for example, you typically use "story points" to relatively assess the effort required to complete different tasks. It is a very deliberate control of the vocabulary of the situation not to estimate work with hours, work days, or dollars.

The point is to make it abstract and keep the focus on relative sizes, because people get distracted when you use a real unit of time. If you say a task can be done in four days, you may get questions about why it can't be done in three. You also get dragged into discussions about duration as opposed to effort. You might get a question about which days will be used for the work. Every single one of these questions shows the questioner trying to get too deep into managing the team's work. Agile's "story points" concept is intentionally designed to structure not just the work, but the discussion about the work, in a certain way.

If you can get your stakeholders to use your vocabulary, and therefore your world view and your rubric for measuring project success, you will have your communications, work, and objective all aligned. That's a pretty good start to achieving success.

The vocabulary of the project is something that should be consciously considered when the project is being organized. It becomes part of the project's brand and its personality, and can have a very real role in assessing a project's success.

Where We Come From

Part of a project's brand, not to mention its own sense of identity, comes from the project's history. Even an apparently "new" project can have one. Did it get spun off from another initiative? Has the same thing been tried four times before, only to fail? Was it inspired by a notable presentation?

The project's history can give the project a sense of mission, even destiny. It might spawn an "us against the world" tone, a "they said it couldn't be done" tone, or an "everyone's counting on you" tone.

The early days of any project often have a different feel, something that is often lost as the project gains speed. Maybe everyone on the team was in a single conference room, or in a basement somewhere. The rules were different, the tone was different. Maybe certain inspirational figures - a business stakeholder or a technical architect - were frequently present and more approachable.

On the other hand, maybe the old days weren't so good. There was no funding, no direction, crazy hours, or a boss who didn't know what he was doing. Maybe everyone's happy those days are gone.

As a project leader, it's up to you to foster the positives out of the project's dawn, while improving on the negatives.

Chapter Wrap-up

You have a personal brand based on your experience and reputation.

It's important to be deliberate about your personal brand. Own it, shape it, and use it while establishing your professional identity.

Your project will also develop a brand. This will affect how your project is viewed and reacted to, but is also something you can influence as a project leader.

Part of a project's brand is to own the vocabulary of its activities and success.

Getting Things Done

Chapter 4: Daring to Change Things

Chapter Summary

A project leader needs to understand his or her environment, identifying what needs to change in order to be successful.

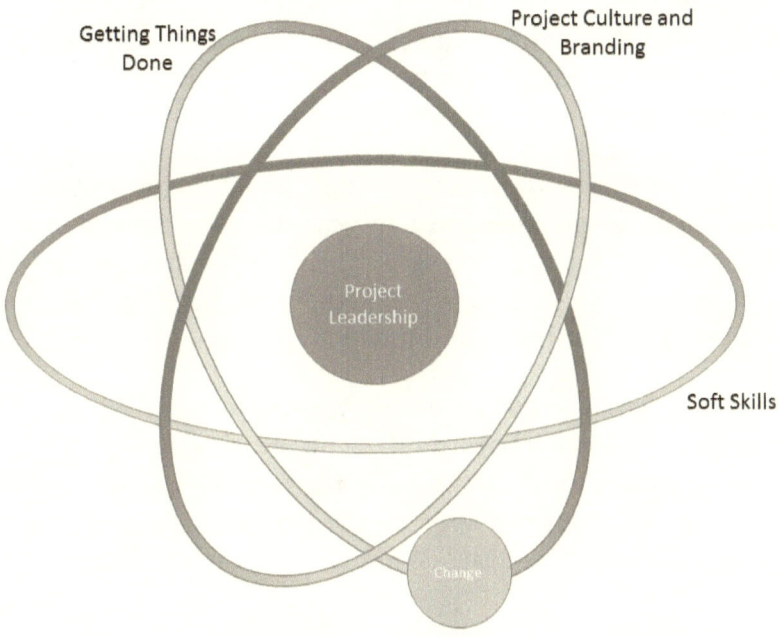

No Sacred Cows

A major part of being a project leader is daring to change things. In the previous couple of chapters, we've discussed managing project cultures. In the next few chapters we'll discuss project structures, methodologies, business constraints, and changing perspectives, and we'll give a reality check to project scheduling. Identifying opportunities for change and making the change happen are two absolutely vital activities for a project leader.

Imagine you're discussing a project that's about to get started. Someone's already sketched out a project charter. They're in the process of assembling the rest of the team. A draft work plan was in the budget request. Now they just need you, the project manager, to come in and make it all work.

In an entirely hypothetical situation, you'd scream at every sentence in the previous paragraph. The project charter? I need to be a part of that! Assembling the team? I didn't approve that! I didn't even approve the team org chart. A work plan? A budget request? What if I don't agree with them?

Do you really expect me to take what you've handed me and succeed at delivering this project? When I didn't have any input on anything at all?

The person discussing the project with you probably wouldn't say it quite this way, but they might want to: "Yes, that's exactly what we expect. Now get your butt on board and do what we tell you."

What's more, most of us have accepted exactly that.

Now, I'm not advocating that you be a pain in the rear end, a project leader prima donna who only insists on doing things your way.

And in the hypothetical situation I just described, in the real world, all of those constraints have been discussed for months. They weren't just imagined. They were put together with people who also have experience and insight. There's probably some value there.

What's more, in the two hours you might be reviewing this information as someone is interviewing you to be the project lead, you probably won't have enough time to really see what works and what doesn't about the set-up. That time will come in about three weeks.

Your job as a project leader is to continue to build a picture in your head about your project. Does the team have what it needs to deliver the objective? Is the objective achievable technically, budget-wise, or on schedule? Are there things outside the project's grasp that impact its ability to deliver?

Every piece of information you get goes into that evolving equation. As the project leader, you've got your hand on the "Emergency Stop" button. When you don't like how the answers stack up, it's up to you to recommend a change.

Making Changes vs. Making Do

It's part of the American mind-set to deal with imperfect circumstances. We applaud improvisation. We cheer when someone makes something out of nothing. We rank the overachiever who overcame every obstacle higher than the perfectly prepared professional.

Remember the story of Apollo 13? We've made a folk-tale out of how engineers figured out how to get a round air filter into a square filter receptacle.

On the other hand, we also celebrate people who take a principled stand. If the plane won't fly, we expect someone to take that unpopular position, no matter how many dignitaries are in attendance to watch the test flight.

So where do we go as project leaders?

A friend of mine who had been in the Army told me about being on maneuvers in West Germany. Americans were in awe of the German trucks. They were in beautiful shape, perfectly engineered, and awesomely maintained. And the Germans? Were they proud of their trucks? Well, they were, but they were also in awe of the American trucks. They were models of the American frontier spirit of using anything available to get things done.

The fact is, we should admire both. We should appreciate the perfectly prepared project with ample resources, delivering with machine efficiency. We should equally admire the project, strapped for resources and hampered in every way, that manages to deliver against all odds. Neither is morally superior.

What you have to realize as a project manager is that you won't always get what you want. You'll have to make do, and encourage your team to work through the disappointment and anger they may feel about it. You need to be able to identify the absolutely critical thing that's needed, and plant your flag on it.

To use the military metaphor, that's the hill you'll want to die on.

I discuss some of this more in a future chapter on project rescue, but I'll dwell here for a moment on knowing what changes are critical.

In a particular project in my experience, the project was already in rescue mode when I got to it. I tried to help it limp along. That was me making do, trying to use the minimal resources to accomplish the objective. After a number of weeks, however, I identified some key ingredients which were missing.

The project team had no documented requirements. We'd pretended we were close to being finished, but in fact, we had no idea. It was a mess. Time to start over.

Given that situation, the team had the wrong resources. Also an item to take a stand on.

This was a good experience, but in retrospect, I didn't go far enough. I was still letting myself be blocked in by certain expectations.

The schedule was the worst part of it. Everyone insisted that the project had to have a new schedule. Communications to clients would be based on it, after all. I dutifully built a schedule, even though nobody else would support it. Nobody believed in it. I didn't believe in it myself.

Since I didn't know what would happen if I was honest about the schedule, I swore we could do it.

Here's a tip: if you're the only person on a project saying something can be done, and even you have doubts, you're probably better off being honest about the situation.

Not only did I need to change the project team and its work approach, I should have forced a change in the need for a schedule. We should have looked for some way to move the project forward incrementally, not letting it get out of control, even though we couldn't be sure when it would be complete.

Making Changes

So we've established a couple of things so far:

*   A project leader is responsible for identifying the
        changes necessary for a project's success.

*   A project leader has to figure out when to take a stand
        and when to make do

So how do you make it happen?

Most projects don't have anything built into their governance
structure about how to make revolutionary changes. The
stakeholders want to hear that things are on automatic:
everything's humming along well, there are no issues which
require their attention, and the budget and schedule are
looking good. No one wants to hear, "We've got an issue that
we have to discuss."

Here are the steps I recommend:

*   Get help

*   Be prepared

*   Communicate thoroughly

*   Make it happen

*   Check back on the results

By the way, these steps don't just apply to massively urgent
crisis situations. They apply equally to much smaller changes,
and can help any project shift go much more smoothly.

Getting Help

You may be a project leader, but it doesn't mean you should make every hard decision yourself or take on every difficult task without any assistance.

Whatever the change is, start by getting help. Talk through the change with a colleague, a mentor, a boss, or other team members. I prefer a mix, talking with people who are very involved along with people who are aware of what I'm doing but are not necessarily personally impacted.

I talk to them about the concern that's leading to the change and why my proposal addresses that concern. I also talk about other options and why I like my proposal best. Would they do the same thing in my situation? Am I missing something? Am I possibly overreacting to a situation that will solve itself?

I also ask about ideas on communicating the change, or tweaks to make on the proposal. I learn something from everyone, and polish the plan and the message based on those contributions.

Be Prepared

You're asking for a change to something about the project. Either it's a condition that was created before you got there, or you were part of making it happen. You need to get your story straight: why are you asking for a change? Why now?

Furthermore, you need to know what your proposal will cost, what problem it will solve, and what the stakes are.

This may be a fairly simple situation - you're asking for a minor schedule change or an additional resource. Or maybe it's very complex or serious, and you're considering quitting the project if your proposal isn't accepted.

Either way, you should also develop what's called in negotiation BATNA - Best Alternative To a Negotiated Agreement. If your proposal isn't accepted, what's going to happen? What's your plan B (and plan C, and plan D)?

In all likelihood, by the time you've got any kind of proposal together, you've also covered plans B, C, D, and any others. You just didn't like them very much. You'll want to have them in your hip pocket (if not your PowerPoint slides), not only to show that you came prepared, but also because maybe someone else has an idea that can rescue them and turn them into a good idea.

Communicate

Whatever you're doing, it isn't going to happen if you don't tell someone else about it.

Get the right people in the right place and give them the information they need.

A key part of the message is what the stakes are. Hopefully, most of the time you're discussing issues where the world is not currently on fire, but you see the need to make a change. Also, I'm hoping that, in most cases, you're not preparing the nuclear option if your proposal isn't accepted. You need to be clear on what issues you're dealing with and how you're addressing them.

It's entirely possible that you'll hit some problem that's big and hairy. It could be so big and hairy you don't even know what you could do about it. You may have been told never to present an issue without having a proposed solution for it, and generally I follow that rule myself.

So what do you do when you're stuck?

The main answer is not to do this during the communication stage. Do it during the "getting help" stage. It might be the same people (i.e., project stakeholders), but you'll want to be clear about the issue and the stakes, and that you're looking for assistance.

If you think any of your stakeholders are not going to be supportive of your impassioned plea for assistance, you might want to leave them out of this stage, and only go to them when you've got something to propose. You don't always just want to talk to "yes men", but when you're looking for a solution to a hairy problem, you need to talk to people who can constructively focus on the problem.

Critical to the communication is to stress that you're doing this to be inclusive and open. You don't want your team or your stakeholders running for cover every time they hear you discussing making changes to the project. Instead, you want to give the message that change is natural, intended to be beneficial, and is under control.

Making It Happen

There are two main things to think about when putting a change into effect.

First, there's the simple timing of it. Can you fit it into the project's current cadence, or do you have to overturn the cadence? Some of your changes will have inherent impacts on your project's rhythm and schedule, and you'll have no choice but to prepare to re-baseline it.

Second, how do you communicate the change to the team? Depending on the nature of the change, you might want to cover it during one on one conversations or during a team discussion. You'll need to have a sense for the changes and

how your team members will respond. Even apparently
neutral changes might be taken badly.

Significantly, you should have a one-on-one discussion for any
change which appears focused on an individual or impacts a
specific person greatly. A change to someone's role, rolling
someone off the project, de-emphasizing a functional area that
they're the expert on - any of these directly impact someone
and you'd be better off talking to them face to face before the
rest of the team knows.

It's easy to think of the obvious situations for a one-on-one.
Don't forget that some situations might be pretty subtle. For
instance, if you were communicating a change where one
person was being promoted to new role, it might seem like that
was the person who ought to get the heads-up. There might be
others on the team who feel left out or passed over, however, so
it might be worth handling that message with private
discussions.

Another factor in the messaging is your own communication
style. If you feel like you can deliver delicate messages better
one-on-one than in a group, by all means take that approach.
If you feel like you can build off the message to a positive team
bonding moment, then get everyone together for the discussion.

Checking Back
As with any change you make, you'll want to take stock of the
impact down on the road. A week, two weeks, three months -
whatever time intervals might have been meaningful to the
change, you should consider the impact of the change.

It's also worth making a small point about the change, possibly
in the course of regular communications. For example, "Hey,
Sally has really worked out in her new role", "The change in

project calendar has really made it easier on the team", and so on. This should include the not-so-positives as well, like, "We're not seeing the uplift we expected yet from this change", or "Joe's still finding his footing in his new role".

This not only indicates that you're paying attention to your changes, it also normalizes the idea of change in the project. We do things, we change them, we evaluate the changes. It's how we work. It's nothing to be afraid of.

Chapter Wrap-up

Being a project leader means daring to make the changes
necessary for project success.

You will often be faced with a delicate choice of accepting the
conditions you're working in and wanting to change them.

Key activities in implementing project changes are:

*   Get help

*   Be prepared

*   Communicate thoroughly

*   Make it happen

*   Check back on the results

Chapter 5: Doing Things Differently
Chapter Summary
A project leader doesn't just set the tone and direction for a project. He or she also can play a significant role in helping the project accomplish its goals and move past obstacles.

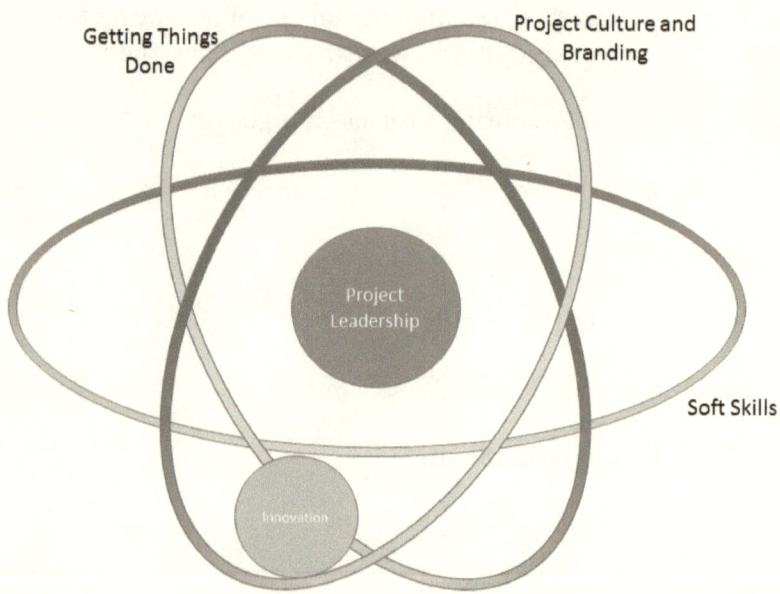

Messing With the Methodology

Some people frown on messing with a methodology. If there's a standard way of doing things, tweaking it can only end in tears. After all, if you're permitted to change it to suit yourself, then it wouldn't be standard. What makes you think you know better than somebody who spent years working on this methodology?

I've used countless methodologies in my career. I've also been part of a team that created a major methodology, and created a couple of small-scale methodologies custom to meet client needs. Every single time, everybody involved agreed that sometimes the methodology needs to be adjusted to suit the circumstances.

There's still validity in the concern of random or uneducated changes. Just as you don't start playing jazz until you actually know what makes the music work, you'd be unwise to make significant changes to a methodology without a good grounding in the subject.

Usually you'll find a specific issue comes up, and the logical solution is to change the methodology. A certain deliverable is unnecessary, certain steps should be done in a different order, or something needs to be added. You'll see those things come up all the time, and you'll probably make the change without even thinking to yourself, "Wow! I just changed the methodology! Do you think I'll get in trouble for that?"

You can also consciously change a methodology, or design one specific to your project's requirements. This may seem like unnecessary work. After all, what are the values of a methodology? First, it includes all the reasonable steps for project completion. Second, someone else already spent the time to figure out all those steps. Why waste your project's time on redoing a methodology?

A couple of reasons. First, a methodology is a great tool when your project fits it perfectly. If you have a project that's out of the ordinary, though, you end up following a path that's not right for you. If you can see this ahead of time, it's worth taking the time to do that customization.

Second, sometimes you have a project that simply demands creativity. You've got a tough problem to crack, and you need ideas that are so out of the box, you can't see the box from where you're standing. Most methodologies don't have a step labeled "Be creative here", so you have to set the stage for it.

The crucial part of getting a team to be creative is to tell them it's okay. Even better, tell them that you expect it. Tell them you want them to be creative, and stand back and watch the ideas charge towards you. You'll probably want to make other changes to support operations in "creative mode" also.

So what's on the table for change? It should be everything!

Location and Facilities
You may not have much choice about where your project is housed, but it's worth asking about. Projects - especially larger ones - may be too large to simply shoehorn into some available cubicles. If you can get involved in the process, you may be able to influence your location and how the team's space is set up.

Here are some questions to ask when you're looking at this.

*   What other groups or departments do we need to be
        close to?

*   Is it a good thing to be on our own, away from day to day operations, or is it a bad thing?

*   How big will the team be? How will the team use its space?

*   Does the team have any special requirements for its space? Does it need special tools or equipment?

Here's another way to look at it: does your project need dedicated space at all? It's kind of a fundamental assumption that teams work best when everyone is one place. Depending on other aspects of your team's style of participation, your space needs might change.

We often assume that a "project" consists of a certain number of people, with a core team of people who are 100% dedicated to the project. Lots of (smaller) projects don't look like that at all. Even larger projects might not fit that model, either. In other circumstances, dedicated project space with work areas for every team member might not be cost effective or very useful.

Similarly, where are your people? "Virtual" teams are becoming far more common. For a virtual team, the focus needs to be on virtual space: that is, the tools they can use to communicate, collaborate, and build a team ethos without actually being in one place.

How about a hybrid situation? Perhaps you have a mix of full-time and part-time resources, some people in one location, some virtual. You might still want to have office space, but recognizing that everyone will use it differently, you'll want it to be fairly flexible.

Work Planning

All right, so now we've sorted out where everyone's going to sit. What are they working on?

Work plans represent the holy writ of methodologies. The Gantt chart was a major advancement in system operations. The PERT chart also has its place. The work breakdown structure (WBS) is probably the most referenced document in the PMBOK guide.[1] It is absolutely fundamental that a project have a plan. That plan also needs dates, assignments, and dependencies.

This doesn't mean that any of these standard representations of work is the best way for your project to talk about its work.

One of the first things I do on a project is develop a mind map (also called a brainstorming diagram) of everything related to the project. A mind map is a visual representation of anything, showing a central idea with its components branching off in spokes to ever decreasing levels of detail.

The mind map helps me see everything there might be to worry about. I'll look at it and then identify some items as not being within my project's scope. Then I can use the mind map to build the work plan. A mind map isn't a work plan, but it can show information in ways a traditional work plan can't. For example, a mind map can more usefully show recurring activities or permanent operations, because it is not tied to sequence or calendar.

Sometimes I use the mind map only to organize my initial thoughts about a project, and to begin developing the WBS.

---

[1] *A Guide to the Project Management Body of Knowledge*, Project Management Institute, 2013.

Some readers may have already noticed a remarkable similarity between the sample mind map and a WBS; the difference is that the WBS covers the project scope, while the mind map can go beyond that to include other project success factors. Besides organizing the work, I sometimes continue to use a project mind map to track status.

Project Process and Daily Operations

With the bigger picture of project work taken care of, we can think about what happens every day.

Take status meetings. Please.

Status meetings are so vilified in American business that they're a standing joke in "Dilbert" cartoons and other media as well.

Usually, status meetings are useful so that people who are more removed from the day to day workings of things can learn what everyone has been doing. Personally, I find this very useful. However, this often means that a whole team's time is taken up to be of service to one person. Perhaps the value of the communication can be argued, but wouldn't it be better if *everyone* got something out of the experience?

The Scrum development methodology has the approach of a daily "scrum" meeting with everyone on a team. This is typically a smaller group, representing people who are influenced directly by each other's work. It should be, ideally, a fifteen minute meeting. Everyone briefly reports what they worked on the day before, what they'll work on today, and what impediments they have. For impediments, the point is not to resolve them there and then, but for someone to speak up and say, "I can help you with that. Let's talk after the scrum".

The objective of the scrum is all-way communication, especially to address impediments. It's intended to be a brief check-in. Often, the team will physically stand up during the meeting (a symbolic representation of the intended brevity), and the meetings may even be called stand-ups.

What's so radical here? The radical idea is that the scrum approach can be used in other settings. It doesn't have to be used only for development projects. Imagine a process design project, a marketing campaign, or the requirements identification phase of a development project that will use a waterfall methodology. These could all benefit from a daily check-in.

Another area that can use a process adapted from other circumstances is the assignment of work.

In most cases, this seems pretty basic. The work plan says what role does what work. People have specific roles on the project, so they do the work belonging to that role. The project manager manages the work assignments. This seems so basic, how could there be any benefit to changing it?

There are several reasons to take a non-traditional approach to this.

First, there is the resource loading of work. One of the major challenges to project managers is to make sure that everyone on the team is fully occupied. This is usually done by estimating tasks in detail and then assigning them in the work plan so that everyone has about the same work load. The resource plan usually makes it about a week before it has to be completely redone. All it takes is one task to fall behind or have a revised estimate, and the resource loading is all wrong.

If you have independent tasks that can be done by multiple people on the project with roughly equal quality, then the alternate approach is to establish a pool of work. The team then draws from that pool when they are ready for a new task. This idea from Kanban production (adapted to some forms of Agile or iterative development) effectively manages the resource loading. As a project leader, you can then focus on the team's overall volume of work and how fast it completes it (sometimes called a velocity). As with the scrum meeting, this approach can be adapted to non-development projects as long as the work being done meets the necessary requirements.

A second reason to take a new approach is preference and aptitude. Some people may prefer one specific functional area or segment of a task. They may be better at it than other work, have a special talent for it, or simply enjoy it more. Besides the Kanban approach mentioned above, there are other ways you could enable work assignment to match preferences. For example, rather than assigning tasks as the project manager, have a meeting where you discuss the work that needs to be done in the next day or week. For each task, let people volunteer for tasks.

You could even find a way to do this without a meeting. You could use a web site or other tool for people to bid on tasks, maybe using some sort of point system, or maybe based on their estimate of how long it will take for them to complete the task.

Note that with any of these alternative approaches, everyone has to buy into it. Ideally, you're building a project culture where people accept that they have committed to completing a task when they claim it or bid on it. The process should build ownership in the work. It's not work "assigned", with an estimate that came on a stone tablet. It's work that the team member chose, committing to completion based on their own estimate.

A third reason is cross-training. Rather than always assigning the most appropriate or most skilled resource to a task, some tasks could be assigned to give people a chance to learn a new area.

Project Roles

The process of work assignment leads to a consideration of how you can revolutionize project roles. The concept of roles is probably even more fossilized in project management lore than work plans. It's endemic to our corporate organizations, our sports, our entire culture.

People have a role to play on a team. Some people are quarterbacks, some people are linemen. Some people sit on the bench and wait for someone to get hurt. If everyone plays their role, the team wins.

This concept may be core to sports, where it usually makes sense. If a soccer team don't grasp their different roles, a soccer game looks like a "herd ball" game of six-year olds.

It's also a fundamental concept to our economy. We consider specialization to be an indicator of cultural progress and economic efficiency. If we all have to be equally good at farming, hunting, and making baskets, we'll all be equally mediocre. How about we let the really good hunters just focus on that, while the people who make awesome pottery stick to that?

Here's the secret ingredient to the role model: it assumes that the roles and their responsibilities are independent of each other. If I'm the village basket maker, I can sit there making baskets all day. You come back from the hunt and I trade you some baskets for some meat. No problem.

But what if I'm not making baskets, but spears? I need to know something about hunting, don't I? Otherwise, I'm probably making lousy spears. If they're not lousy, at the least they're not the best spears they could be.

Think how much better the process works if Fred the hunter takes Bob the spear maker out on the hunt. Bob sees how his spears work in a real world application, and quickly identifies how they can be better. Then Bob shows Fred how he makes a spear. Maybe Fred has a suggestion about how to make the spear better. Maybe the spear is fine, but Fred isn't throwing it right. It gets better because they share their knowledge.

Now think about your project. What can you do with roles? Here are some approaches to think about:

*   Job swapping: do one role for six months, then move on to a new role.

*   Embedding: put someone into another team so they understand how that team works and what work they do.

*   Teaming or pairing: put two people together and have them work on every task as a team, each bringing their different perspectives and experiences.

*   Super-specialist: if a role has multiple functions, and someone is really good at one or two of them but not the others, have them specialize in what they're good at.

*   Rover: counter to the super-specialist, what if someone has skills all over the place, with a really good view of

how things tie together? Think about making them a
roving trouble-shooter, helping people on any kind of
issue that comes up.

A word regarding the RACI matrix. RACI stands for
Responsible, Accountable, Consulted, and Informed, and the
matrix is commonly used as a way to document roles and
responsibilities on a project. It's also one of my least favorite
project management artifacts.

First, it's confusing. I have yet to hear a practical distinction
between Responsible and Accountable that doesn't leave people
confused and frustrated. A common definition is that
Responsible means who's doing the work and Accountable
means who approves it, and that would seem to be clear
enough. The definition doesn't stop there, though. The A (for
Accountable) is also defined as being the person who is
ultimately answerable for completion of a task or duty. In
actual practice (and possibly because the tool is grossly mis-
used), the distinction is easily lost. The A and R are often
assigned to the same person or role, or people have a hard time
finding the difference between responsible and accountable. If
you must use a RACI matrix, I'd suggest simply combining A
and R to save yourself the time discussing the philosophical
distinction between the roles.

Second, the RACI matrix enables and encourages people to
hide in their boxes. Yes, you should know who has
responsibility for what, but it's often simply used to declare a
limit to one's own responsibility. In project leadership, we're
looking for people who will constructively reach across
organizational lines in the interests of project success. A RACI
matrix doesn't help us with that.

There's a good reason for well-defined roles, just as there's value in using a standard methodology. People like to know where they stand. However, with unique needs and adaptable team members, you can take a creative approach to roles that can really deliver value to the project.

Project Documentation and Deliverables

Another trope in the world of project management is the shelf full of project documentation, laboriously assembled at great expense and never opened, ever again. The formula for the elixir of life could be in there, but it will never be found, because no one will ever open those binders.

Here are my first two principles of project documentation:

1.   If no one will refer to it, it's useless.

2.   A task isn't done until you've told someone you've done it.

So, you have to tell someone you completed a deliverable (designed a process, built a web site, invented a gadget) and leave a record of how it was done, but you have to do it in such a way that it's actually useful to somebody.

Sounds like another opportunity to get creative!

I think it's become relatively common to create documentation in a work of a wiki, a website that's constantly being updated by its users. In theory, then, the completion of any task includes updating the wiki so it reflects the new status of the project and its objectives.

This certainly handles principle #1. As to the first, the wiki's online structure makes it easier to search and reference. Also, it eliminates those gargantuan photocopying costs.

That's one approach, although it's a relatively minor modification to the actual documentation itself. It's still a whole lot of writing.

So why not do a video showing what you did? The web is full of video tutorials. Most of them seem to be things like playing the guitar, making craft projects, and beating difficult bosses in World of Warcraft, but some of them are useful things like how to do certain tricks in Microsoft Excel.

Done well, a video tutorial is a much better record of the work than a written document. Imagine documenting a process, not by a forty-eight pages of swim lane diagrams, but with an actual re-enactment, with different people playing the functional roles in the process.

Joe: "I complete this form, creating this identification number, which I then hand to Sue."

Sue: "I enter the identification number in this other system, and now the two records are linked."

People can see the process hand-offs and get more information about the process itself.

Clearly, some specifications and conditions should still be committed to words. Some things will just be easier to find that way. But you should never overlook the possible advantages of other media: not only can you deliver useful documentation, you may find other benefits that you never expected.

Documentation and training aren't exactly the same thing (as they may have different audiences), but they are still strongly linked. The classical instructor-led training approach isn't always the most effective or efficient, and you should look for ways to improve it.

Indulge me as I provide an example of the benefits of getting radical on training and documentation.

Some years ago I was creating a trimmed-down project management methodology for an IT department. This company had essentially no process whatsoever, so the smallest standardization was likely to be pretty valuable. I worked out the process and the supporting forms, and then prepared to do training for the small department.

I had a couple of weeks to prepare for the training, and I was not looking forward to the task. A standard training presentation would have been about twenty-five slides stepping through the new process, providing examples, and taking questions. Two hours talking about methodology ... it would be dull, and that was just for me, who'd be doing all the talking.

I hit upon another solution. Since I have a hobbyist interest in tabletop games, I would create a game. It would have to reflect every step in the methodology, and the participants would have to actually accomplish a task during the session. The ideas started to come together...

There still needed to be a lecture component to the training, just to explain what we were doing and what the value was. I decided I'd spent an hour on that, and then we'd go to the hands-on segment. I found an educational supply store where I picked up three identical Junior Erector sets for making a helicopter. The task would be for the teams to build the helicopter. I tried to add a cost component by putting a price on every piece of the helicopter, and permitting the teams to modify the design (thus saving money by eliminating parts). In the end, that didn't work so well, but it was a lesson learned for the next time.

Anyway, I put everything together and was all ready for the training. My manager was out on vacation all this time, and I had no team members working on this with me, so I was performing without a safety net. I did take the precaution of briefing the CIO on my plans, and he didn't have any objections, so away we went!

Much to my surprise, the lecture segment of the training was incredibly popular. The concept of standard steps in running a project was enthusiastically received, and there were many engaged and constructive questions. I could easily have spent the entire two hours on this, but I had toy helicopters to get built. I explained the task, handed out the Erector sets, and the teams got to work.

This is where the unexpected benefits started coming in. Normally you think of training as a very one-directional thing: information is going one way and (hopefully) absorbed by the audience. When you do something interactive, though, information starts heading back the other direction. I wished I'd been prepared for this so I could have coached the CIO more on what to watch for.

First of all, I hadn't done anything to assign seats, so the nine participants sorted themselves into seats. The way they grouped themselves might have been easy to predict, but even that's an indicator of how the team aligns itself.

Second, one group was made up of the PC guy, the network guy, and the phone guy. Each team was supposed to create its own work plan for constructing their helicopter: this team's final step was to tighten all the bolts. That's good - that's exactly the mentality you want out of your hardware guys!

Third, I'd made the instructions for building the helicopter to be a cost component. Personally, I'd tried to make one of the helicopters but I hadn't been able to do it without the instructions. Interestingly, all three teams chose not to pay for the instructions! If I was the CIO, I think I'd have my eyebrows raised at that point.

It turned out that all the teams were successful at assembling the helicopters, even without visual aids. One of the teams told me that their plan had been to try to do it without the instructions, but if they were having problems at the status checkpoint halfway through, they were going to buy the instructions then.

Imagine if your development team didn't bother to look at the requirements documentation until halfway through the build phase of your project!

In the end, the event was a grand success, and I could have planned four hours instead of two for it. I would have liked to have allowed more discussion time at the end for people to compare their experiences, for example.

Still, not only was this one of the most fun things I ever got to do in my job, it was also one of the greatest learning experiences. Nothing can tell you more about how your team works than to see them do a task, together, right in front of you.

That's just one way to get out of the box in business operations and projects. With a nod to a couple of sources[2], when you're looking for a way to change things up, you can ask yourself a few questions to provoke some ideas:

*   What if I make something bigger? Bigger team?

*   What if I make something smaller? Smaller team, shorter project phases?

*   What if I change the order of tasks?

*   What if I change who does what?

You can also look at smaller ideas for changing how to run team meetings or maintain team communications.[3]

[2] "Creative Whack Pack", Roger Von Oech, 1989, and "Thinkpak", Michael Michalko, 2006.

[3] "Visual Meetings", David Sibbet, 2010, and "Visual Teams", David Sibbet, 2011, as example sources of ideas.

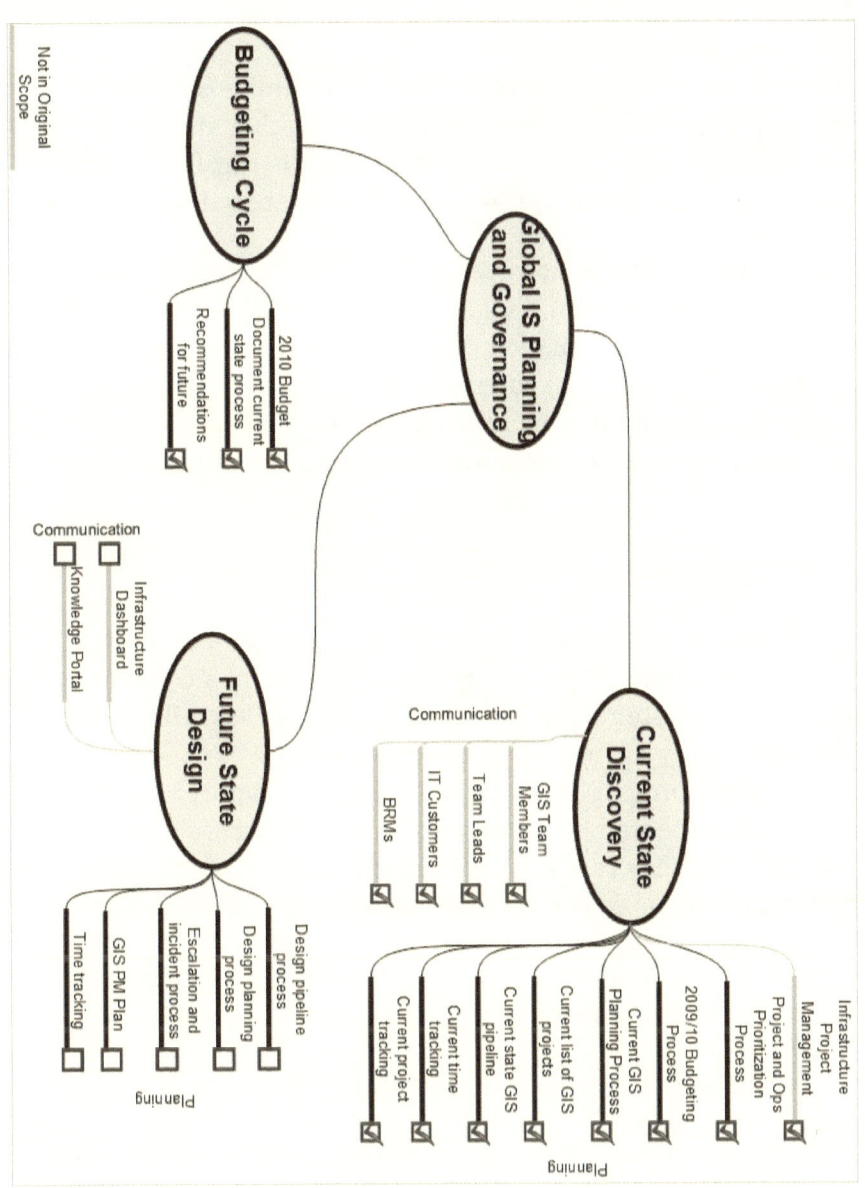

FIGURE 2. EXAMPLE MIND MAP.

Inspired Solutions

A project manager is usually involved in defining the project outcome. Somebody has to schedule the meeting and facilitate the discussion, after all. A project manager is rarely asked for ideas on actually defining the solution or strategy itself.

Being a project leader, however, means offering your expertise and insight in that area. You might not be a specialist in the industry or business function, but you can still bring your background and problem solving techniques to the meeting. You can be part of inspired solutions. You can drive a "Yes, and" attitude. You can set a tone for creativity and can-do optimism.

Let me give you an example of that sort of solution.

I was working with a client to implement an e-procurement system. The idea of this was that an employee of a company could use the system to order products themselves, eliminating the traditionally arduous purchasing processes. Those processes continue to bring critical value to the purchase of direct goods (the items that go into the manufacture of actual products), but they're a waste of time for indirect goods (like office supplies and MRO [maintenance, repair, and operations]).

The traditional purchase process looks something like this:

*   Person A identifies a need to buy something.

*   Person A tells Person B (in Purchasing) what they need, usually in the form of a requisition.

*   Person B gets quotes for the product; a rigorous process would require at least three separate quotes.

*   Person B determines the best quote and creates a
    purchase order.

*   The purchase order is sent to the vendor.

*   The vendor fulfills the order, shipping the product. At
    more or less the same time, but through a parallel set of
    steps, the vendor sends an invoice requesting payment
    for the product.

*   Person C at the purchasing company gets the product at
    the receiving dock. They document that the product
    was received via a receipt.

*   Person D (in Accounts Payable) gets the invoice. They
    match up the purchase order, the receipt, and the
    invoice in what's called a three-way match. If the
    numbers all tie together, they can pay the invoice
    (although an additional approval might still be
    required).

E-procurement creatively attempted to improve this process by
collapsing the first five steps. Person A decides what they need
and can pick it through a catalog in the system. They select it
and an electronic order goes to the vendor. They can do this
because the electronic catalog already has prices associated
with it, thus skipping the quoting step.

If this sounds painfully obvious, it's because it's the way we buy
things on-line today. We also don't usually have personal
purchasing departments (spouses excepted). Companies,
however, do these things because the policies help drive a
separation of duties, which is intended to keep people from
doing bad things without anyone else noticing.

On our project, we still had one obstacle to making this process really smooth. That's the receipt.

For most indirect goods, the shipment doesn't go to a receiving department. The recipient might be in an office that doesn't even have a receiving department, so the purchase usually goes directly to the requester.

While the e-procurement system has a nice page for the requester to log that they received the product, who's going to bother? They've already got their goodies, and the payment really isn't their problem. So no one enters receipts.

But if there's no receipt, we can't do a three-way match. And if we can't do a three-way match, we have a very frustrated person in Accounts Payable. And then we don't pay the vendor, and they never want to send us anything, ever again.

So we came up with a paradigm-shattering idea. What if we didn't bother with the receipt?

Okay, you probably came up with that idea as soon as you read the paragraph saying that no one enters receipts. We still had a problem, though.

In the business world, that receipt is the trigger to pay the invoice. First, you don't pay a bill you haven't received yet. Even then, we can't just go around paying every invoice that comes in the door. We might be getting overcharged, or charged for a product we never got.

So what could we do? With the tone set for finding creative solutions, we came up with the idea of "paying on assumed receipt". Every item in a catalog would have a typical delivery range (1-2 or 5-7 days after the order is received, for example). With a week or so generously added to that range, the system would automatically send a receipt to Accounts Payable when that date was reached. The premise was that if everything went well and the requester got what he wanted, it would be fine to pay for it. If things didn't go well, they'd call the vendor and make a fuss.

After all, think of how you handle things when you order something on-line. You get your box, you open it, you check out what you got. If it's fine, yay! The charge is already on your credit card. If it's not okay, you're on the phone in five minutes complaining to the seller.

So far, so good. We've creatively used the personal requisition paradigm in a business context. The process is simpler but the system requirements are all satisfied. We're rock stars.

Alas, no. It turns out there's something else on the invoice. A couple of things, actually. Taxes and shipping.

Both of these items don't get associated with the product being purchases and often turn out to be values that couldn't be predicted. The old three-way match took care of this by making sure the purchase order, which was supposed to match the quote, already had these numbers. The e-procurement system didn't have them, though.

The shipping and handling problem can be taken care of the way most EBay sellers operate: they establish ahead of time what the charge is going to be, and you have to accept it as part of the sale. You strongly suspect that they're padding the cost to their benefit, but at least you know what it is. The shipping and handling can be added to the product cost, though, solving that problem.

Taxes were another story. Now, for a long time internet purchases were not subject to state sales taxes (or at least,

there was a complicated exemption available). The US
Congress established this exemption in order to give the
internet a boost up. The internet has made good use of it, so
the exemption's gone away. For businesses, though, that
exemption was never there. E-procurement didn't really count
as buying something on-line.

In theory, the taxes could be folded into the price of the product
also, right? Not so fast. The taxes vary depending on where
the product is going, which the vendor doesn't know when they
set the prices in their on-line catalog. Also, the states like to
have itemization of the purchases with their state tax amounts
shown.

This is where we got *really* innovative. We went back to the
states to ask if we could just pay them their sales tax monthly,
rather than on every transaction. That way we could get our
purchases, add them all up, and pay them all at once.
Somewhat to my surprise, we got them to agree. With that
barrier out of the way, our "payment on assumed receipt"
became a reality, and that's what we delivered.

This was pre-Sarbanes-Oxley, so I'm not sure if you could even
do this today. Nevertheless, it shows the sort of creative
thinking that you can foster as a project leader.

In this particular case - and in most cases you may experience -
it's not the project leader who necessarily comes up with the
wildly creative ideas. The project leader can be the shepherd
for ideas, encouraging people to look for solutions and not
assume that certain things are impossible.

Getting Over the Hump

Sometimes your team is near the end, but just can't get across the finish line. Some mysterious error continues to plague the system, some set of process steps just don't fit together right, or the strategic direction seems to have something missing.

This is another place where a project leader can come and differentiate herself from a project manager.

A project manager can nag and chivvy the team to address those final hurdles and meet the project schedule, but doesn't have enough knowledge of what the team is doing to really help. A project leader, on the other hand, can step in and actually contribute.

We often talk about having a fresh set of eyes review a document. The idea is that if you've been staring at the same problem for two days, you can't see anything anymore. You can't tell what's right or wrong. A project leader can come in and provide a fresh perspective.

You still have to have enough knowledge to be useful. I once came along and helped a team member solved a bug by identifying a typo in the code with about one minute of looking at it. That was really a complete fluke, but without programming experience, I wouldn't have even known the sort of things to look for.

Sometimes you provide value by talking through the problem with someone. Having them explain things, step by step, can help them realize something they've missed. If not, your questions can help get closer to the solution.

Why did they do step A? Why is answer B necessarily the answer?

A big value that a project leader offers is the ability to see the big picture.

I'm really not fond of that expression because it's used comparatively. I'm a big picture thinker, so my thoughts are more valuable than yours. Harrumph!

We need people looking at the details. Depending on your preference in quotes, either God or the Devil is in the details. Either way, the details make everything work in the end.

The point is that you need both the vision and the nitty-gritty details for success. What you have as a project leader is the ability to see things at the middle level - not the grand strategy, perhaps - but a slightly more elevated level than a worm's eye view. You can see what everyone on the project is doing and how those activities relate to each other. In the end, you can see how each task fits into the project outcome.

This is a huge role for a project leader. I can't count the number of times I've talked with a team member who was stumped on how to solve a problem, and my conclusion was that they were solving the wrong problem. Have I had a lot of dumb team members? Not at all - I think I've had brilliant people on my teams. The problem is that someone too close to a problem will solve it within parameters that they feel are unchangeable.

As a project leader, you can bring in that new perspective. Perhaps the team member was trying to establish an automated solution to a problem when a manual solution will do. Maybe they're trying to add a product feature that no one has asked for. Quite possibly they're trying to solve an edge case that really doesn't need to be solved. The project leader can step in and say, "No, think smaller on this one. All we need to do is..."

Of course, it's also the project leader's job to say, "You need to think *bigger* on this one. I think you've missed something."

Sometimes an even simpler action is called for. On one occasion I was leading the system test of a major system. A bug had been found, and everything was halted while one person on the team fixed it. I went to her and said, "What can I do to help?"

"I'd really like a latte," she answered. So I walked down the street to a gourmet coffee place and bought her a latte. It blew her mind. She never thought I'd do that - she told me that she'd almost said that as a joke. But it was exactly what she needed, and that support helped her knock off the bug and get us going again.

Chapter Wrap-up

Coming up with new ways of doing things is part of a project leader's role.

Project innovations may occur in:

*   Messing with the methodology; tweaking project
         standards and deliverables to be useful to your project.
         Mix in ideas from other methodologies, change the
         visual appearance of your deliverables, and look at other
         ways to approach the work.

*   Working with your team and stakeholders to come up
         with inspired solutions: a project leader doesn't just
         keep the sheep heading the right direction, but should
         bring experience and insight into the solution of
         business problems.

*   Getting your team to the finish line.

Chapter 6: Real World Project Scheduling
Chapter Summary
A project leader tailors the project schedule and administrative process to support the project objective.

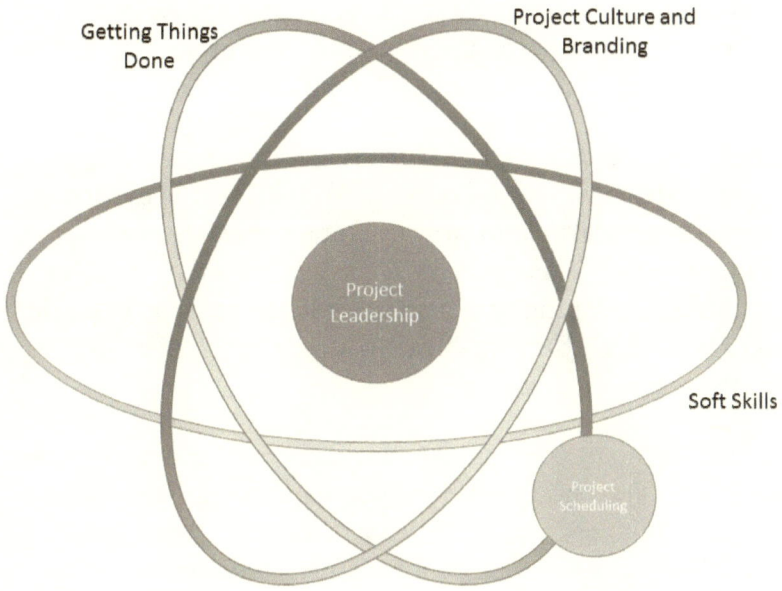

Project Work Plans Equal Project Management

If you ask someone who's not a project manager what project management is, their answer would probably start with managing the work plan. While it's certainly not everything a project manager does, the conventional wisdom has the right idea. Scheduling the project activities, tracking their progress, making work assignments, and managing the project budget is the core of project management and administration.

This might seem like a strangely technical and detailed area to go into when discussing project leadership. But it is exactly because of its central role in project management that I'm addressing it here. The objective is for you to understand the "why" behind developing and managing a project schedule, and for you to remember that this area is as much a subject of deliberate choices as any other.

Project management as a job description came out of schedule management. The Gantt chart is over a hundred years old. Critical path analysis and PERT charts are more than fifty years old. These tools are used for business and information technology projects, civil engineering, scientific research and testing, and home construction. The tools are excellent constructs for managing activities occurring over time, all the better for being independent of the nature of the work being done.

I've even used a Gantt chart for planning my vacation, but maybe I'm just weird.

It's simply fundamental: a project is defined as a "temporary endeavor ... with a defined beginning and end, usually time constrained".[4] With time the critical factor, a schedule is an obvious necessity.

So what are the purposes of the project schedule?

*   Calculate the overall duration of the project, based on the duration of its components

*   Identify the components at a suitable level for management (assignment, status, and time recording)

*   Identify who is responsible for completion for each task

*   Identify the scheduling interaction between project activities

*   Enable reporting on progress against schedule and budget

The worst thing an organization can do with project scheduling is not to have any standard policies or tools at all. That would force every project manager to start from scratch; every project would follow different conventions; and it would be quite likely that meaningful steps could be omitted.

It can also be a problem to over-standardize on policies or tools. A company with a strong Project Management Organization (PMO) may have very specific rules about the contents and structure of a project schedule and the process to use it on a project. You may have noted that I'm wary of iron-clad rules, and this is no exception. As a project leader, you need to weigh the value of the standards against the requirements of your project.

Here are the kinds of standards you may run into in project scheduling, and when you should be cautious of adhering to them.

[4] Official definition of a project from PMI.org, 2015.

Every task has to be broken down to have an estimate no greater than 40 hours

This is based on a couple of principles. First, while effort does not always equal duration, it does mean that you'll often be able to fit the task into a calendar week. This makes task assignment and follow-up easier for the project manager. Second, the logic is that if you can't break a task down to this level, you don't really know what's going on in there. You have higher uncertainty in the estimate, and you're more likely to see the task exceed the estimate.

This isn't a bad rule and the logic is sound. However, recall that most project management rules like this were created in a context of a complex, multiple phase, multiple year development projects. Your project may not require the same task-level rigor to be effectively managed.

Anyhow, what if you really think that a task requires sixty hours, and there's simply no breaking it down? Or there's a set of tasks that collectively add to more than 40: you know what they are, you can separately document them, but it's a well-defined task with low risk? Why create lots of additional work plan lines if it doesn't help you understand what's going on?

Every project plan has to include the same phases and high-level tasks (one-size-fits-all standards)

The idea here is to make sure that standard tasks are included in every plan. This enables projects to be compared against each other. It also means the project can be relatively easily handed off to a different project manager.

Generally, this is a good idea. The idea of creating standards like this is to make project management a repeatable exercise with no surprise for your stakeholders.

Keep in mind, though, that the work plan template was created by human beings, not handed down from a mountain on stone tablets. Unless a PMO (for example) has mandated a standard work plan structure, the standards should be seen as guidelines, especially for less experienced project managers to follow. They should never be simply copied and re-used: you're more likely to forget something unique to your own project if you're trying too hard to adapt to the standard plan.

Consider the contrary examples.

*   Your project is a packaged implementation, whereas the standard assumed custom development.

*   Your project consists of only a segment of the typical work, such as the creation of a set of reports using existing data and an already-implemented reporting tool.

*   Your project is only intended to cover one phase of a standard methodology.

Another case is simply that your project is quite small. A plan is still a good idea, but a 300 line work plan is complete overkill. Slim it down to the point necessary to actually manage the work being done, using judgment about the level of task where attention is needed.

At the other end of the spectrum, a gigantic project might require significant additions to the work plan for items which never appear in a template.

Every plan requires detailed task and resource management, the use of standardized phase gates, and phase containment.

These are all project management best practices. They are critical for the control of large programs, and involve skills that any project manager should be very familiar with.

An organization with standards for these items will usually also have associated estimation guidelines. For example, one company I worked with directed that strictly maintained phase gates automatically applied a 25% contingency to the upcoming phase and a 100% contingency to any phases after that. And, they assumed they would spend it all. The principle was a sound one: if you're doing preliminary system design work for a major custom system, how would you really have any idea what the implementation will cost?

As with the previous rules, these assume a certain scale of project. Your own project may have a different requirement, and you should at least propose consolidating or eliminating actions that do not add value to the project or improve controls.

A significant issue to some people is that these rules all assume a traditional one-phase-at-a-time, first things first methodology. Virtually all over these rules simply don't work for projects that use an iterative development methodology, or for non-system projects that may require more freedom in the flow of work.

What's more, while certain standards are a good idea, it's not necessarily a good idea to mandate an entire methodology regardless of the sort of projects that may come up. I'm a firm believer in using the right tool for the job: some projects are classic candidates for a waterfall approach, while some will be most effectively completed using an iterative approach.

Most important to me is that the choice is based on a *decision*. A methodology or a project schedule template is used not because it was the default, but because it was evaluated as the right thing for the project.

Having standards is still valuable. However, once a company accepts that some of its projects may be done using Agile, Scrum, Lean, or some other form of iterative development, it should also establish standards for applying those methodologies. They should define standard iteration or sprint lengths, expectations for the minimum viable product, and standards on story point usage. You may eventually want to question these rules for your project, but these guidelines will help drive repeatability in project execution while acknowledging that there are different ways to organize work.

Another problem is that many standards are focused on setting a work plan and then managing the work (through structured task assignments), but don't look at the downstream use of the information. What will happen when someone has to log their time against the schedule? How will you do reporting against it?

We'll talk about those questions more in the next section.

Project Leadership in Scheduling

So how do you apply project leadership in scheduling? As with the other topics we've discussed, there are a few basic principles.

* Make sure it adds value

* Make sure it's right for your project

* Understand scheduling as a process: how you build a project work plan will impact what you and the team do downstream

Schedule Design

It might seem odd that to talk about designing a project schedule or work plan (I'll use schedule and plan interchangeably here). Hasn't this problem already been solved? Can't we just use the Gantt chart, PERT chart, Microsoft Project plan, or Excel template we used on another project last year?

It's always sensible to re-use something else if it's applicable, but the point of design is to be deliberate about what you're doing. You can re-use last year's project plan as a starting point, but make sure it answers your own needs.

It may also be that you are not given an option about the tool to use, and you might even be given a standard structure to follow. You will still have questions to answer and options to determine for your design.

The two primary questions you answer in schedule design are what tool or structure to use, and what level of detail to use in the plan.

When I say "tool", I'm referring to the software product being used. Typical products include Microsoft Project, Microsoft Excel, or online task management tools like Team Foundation Server or Jira.

For "structure", I'm referring to the way you actually organize and define the tasks in the plan. For example, you could organize tasks by team, by business function, by phase, and so on, with each approach presenting a different appearance. Also, the level of detail to be documented is a consideration.

First, for the tool or structure to use, you'll need to consider:

* How are you sharing the schedule with team members and other stakeholders?

   A schedule built in an uncommon tool may be difficult to share with others; for example, most of your team may not have access to Microsoft Project.

* Who will be performing updates to the plan?

   If only you or one or two others will be making updates to the plan, it can be built using a tool that only you are familiar with or have access to. If you expect multiple team members to update the plan, you'll want to pick a tool and plan structure that supports the needed technical access and maintenance process you have in mind.

* How does the tool or structure support resource loading?

   For larger projects, a tool should have the ability to assign tasks to individual resources and then analyze the work load by resources. For smaller projects, you might not worry at all about resource loads.

*   How does the tool or structure support your plans for
      time entry and tracking?

      Many people look at the work plan as an end in itself.
      However, if you intend to track the time spent by team
      members at the task level, the tool and structure of the
      plan need to support it. Do you want to have your team
      members potentially assigning time to dozens of
      different tasks? If they only log time against a single
      task, are you getting the reporting information you
      need?

      Also, how will the time get into your plan? Can your
      team members enter it through a feature in the tool
      (such as Microsoft Project Server or Jira), or will you
      need a separate process and tool with the time being
      manually entered?

      It's also possible that you don't want to track time at all,
      in which case none of this will matter. Generally you
      want to track time in some fashion (and it may be
      mandated by your company or project management
      organization), but there are some cases where time
      tracking at the task level is not critical or of high value.
      You should be very confident that it's unnecessary
      before excluding time tracking as a requirement.

*   How does the tool or structure support tracking of
      status by task or deliverable?

      While some work plans are only used to set the course,
      it's generally valuable to keep the schedule up to date
      with status on each line item. Similar to previous
      questions, who will be updating the items? What
      options do you want for status tracking (percent

complete, or indicating state such as not started, in progress, in review, etc.)?

When designing the schedule, you'll want to be thinking about the process for getting status updates, as that will need to be part of your project administrative processes.

* How much schedule analysis do you expect to do? (Examples include critical path analysis and earned value calculations.) How will the approach support this analysis?

On larger and more complex projects, you'll want to rely on your scheduling tool for analysis. With hundreds of tasks in a plan, you won't want to manually review every task to re-calculate your critical path or add up earned value.

On smaller or more straight-forward projects, there may be only a single chain of tasks. You won't be doing much analysis on a project like that, so it won't be a requirement for the tool you choose.

* What tools match my planned methodology?

A heavily task-driven planning tool like Microsoft Project is designed for waterfall style projects and does not well support iterative development models. It can be used, but many of its more valuable features will not be of any use.

On the other hand, some tools are focused directly on team work assignment rather than planning, and are therefore more useful for Agile or iterative projects rather than a waterfall project.

Familiarity is also a reasonable thing to consider. Besides any consideration of standards compliance, your team or company's comfort with the tool is also important.

One other part of work plan design deserves a tangent of its own. In a case where you may have multiple work streams or other parallel, non-integrated work, you should consider whether to have one work plan or multiple. In particular, if you have project managers who will be responsible for their separate areas and their overall work cadence may be independent, it may make sense to have separate work plans.

In the end, what's important is the use of tools that stakeholders and project participants alike can understand. It's more important to have the shared knowledge of the plan and its status than it is to use a particular tool.

After answering these questions, you should assemble a proposal which includes the tool, plan structure, and sketches of the team processes for time entry and task management. This should be approved by your project's stakeholders or steering committee.

Project Estimation

Closely related to the project schedule is estimating the duration and effort required by task and phase. The collected estimate will be a major component to determining your project budget.

There are classically (not to mention logically) two ways to establish an estimate: from the top down and from the bottom up.

Bottom up is favored from a technical point of you. It just makes sense that if you can identify all of project's tasks, define the relationship of the tasks to each other, and estimate their required effort independently, you will have a more accurate and intellectually honest answer.

Top-down has its points as well. Sometimes you don't have the time to complete a work plan and task-level estimate. You might be trying to compare different scope options, for instance. It might be sufficient to judge the number of resources required versus a particular duration per phase and arrive at an estimate that way. The top-down approach does have a notable weakness in that it requires the estimator to have sufficient experience to make appropriate estimates. If the person doing the estimation doesn't have the right experience, the estimate could be horribly inaccurate.

Here's a radical idea: do both!

First of all, the two approaches can actually be used as a check against each other. Obviously, a bottom-up estimate can highlight a gross mis-estimate in the top-down, but the reverse is also possible. A common issue with bottom-up estimates is that minor over-estimates (or padding) applied in every task, along with a conservative sequencing of the tasks, will end up ballooning the project schedule and overall cost. A project that a seasoned program manager judges to be three months in length might be estimated as six months, and it's the comparison (along with professional experience) that can bring the estimates back in line.

Second, it's not unreasonable to establish broad estimates for the phases themselves (through top-down estimating), and then flesh out the details through bottom-up estimating.

A common scenario is that higher-level estimates will be developed during a budget or proposal process and the project stakeholders will expect the detailed plan to be derived, at least in part, from the estimates that were used for project approval. The detailed approach will be desired to establish a schedule that will be tracked and reported against, but high-level status can be shown against the broader estimate.

Another approach is the use of an iterative development methodology or other case where the exact work within the project can't be specified at the outset. A general program plan is still necessary, however. The top-down estimate can be used in that case to provide a framework for the project activity. A slight change to that is to establish a time box for each stage of the project; having the top-down estimate gives the time boxes a closer connection to the actual time required.

One other item on estimating: there's also an art to how detailed estimates are determined. It's been shown that the most accurate estimates are arrived by a project manager working alongside the team member who will do the task. At the very least, you should consider involving a team lead or peer who has more experience with the activity that will be done. Unless you've personally been doing this sort of work very recently, you'll want to avoid being the sole source of a task estimate.

Defining a Task

I mentioned earlier the common rule that any task representing over 40 hours of work should be broken down into multiple tasks. That's far from the only rule (or rule of thumb) that appears in the definition of tasks in a work plan.

In general, you want to make the tasks clear in scope and direction. How many times have you written a work plan or checklist, then gone back to it several weeks later and been unable to recall what the point of one of entries was?

Beyond that, the rules you follow in defining tasks should enable the assignment and tracking of tasks that you'll be doing for the project. Here are some ground rules I recommend:

*   Tasks should follow a consistent format which makes the action and objective clear.

   One approach is to make task descriptions verb-driven, as in "Document the work plan rules of thumb" rather than "Work plan rules of thumb".

   In iterative development, user story descriptions typically follow the structure of, "As a <role>, I want to be able to <perform a system function>".

*   Every task should have *exactly one* associated deliverable (a document or work product).

   For example, "Establish issues and risk logs" would theoretically have two deliverables and therefore should be two tasks.

   If you think a task has no deliverable, ask yourself why you're doing it and how you will know that the task is complete.

   An additional value of having a deliverable associated with a task is that it becomes a definition of done. This is a common part of a user story, but equally valuable in waterfall work task.

*   Every task should have *exactly one* assigned resource (if possible).

   As with the having one deliverable per task, so should you strive to have only one assigned resource. It makes it clearer who is responsible for task completion and also forces more thought on what the task actually is.

For example, if you have a business analyst and a developer jointly assigned to a task, you could probably divide the task by the relative functions each is performing.

The one exception I can see to this is when you have two or more people plainly working in collaboration, and not just on this particular task. An example would be in a case where you're using pair programming.

You should be a stickler for this rule when it comes to time tracking. If other people can apply time to a task, you will lose clarity on what effort was needed for the actual task. This will screw up your project analysis and comparison to any other projects. And by the way, this means you, too: your own time should not be randomly assigned to project tasks.

How about in the case where one team member assists another on a task? It depends: if the tracking of time is critical, I'd create a separate task for the assistant. If the tracking isn't so critical, or the assistance did not have an adverse effect on the completion of that person's tasks, I wouldn't track it at all.

* Don't include meetings except as milestones. I don't mean to say that meetings aren't work. They're just clutter on a work plan. Again, I'd say there are exceptions based on how you want to define "meeting". A workshop with a specific, desired outcome related to project deliverables would be a reasonable thing to put on a work plan; a status meeting or general issue resolution meeting would not qualify as an exception.

* Avoid non-tasks like "consider", "review", or "verify". These often end up on work plans to reflect the time difference between the completion of a draft deliverable

and the day that it is actually presented. They also usually precede meetings (see previous point). However, they're difficult to assign, estimate, or verify as complete. If you must include a step like this, treat it formally: the deliverable of the task (such as a sign-off) should be a document indicating the completion.

* Don't include operational, on-going responsibilities. You may be tempted to include things like development operations in a work plan in order to make your resource plan look right. You might also be tempted to include some vague "Provide project support" or "Manage project team" tasks for project managers or administrators. If the task does not have a single point-in-time completion, then it's really not a project action and should not be on the plan.

    That doesn't mean your project won't still be responsible for it. It just means it shouldn't be on your work plan. Don't forget to account for that when you reconcile your top down and bottom up estimates!

Using the Project Schedule

The project schedule is of little value if you just write it and then put it in a drawer. It needs to be integrated with the other activities of managing the project, and it needs to be kept up to date. Connected activities include:

* Time tracking

* Project and deliverable status

* Re-baselining

* Project analysis

Throughout the life of your project, you should continually verify that the project schedule enables these other tasks and reconsider its design if it is not.

Ultimately, the work plan is a tool like so many others you have at your disposal. If it does not serve a purpose, then it took up time you could have used on something with real value.

Chapter Wrap-up

Make sure your project's scheduling standards and schedule constructively support your project's needs.

Understand that project scheduling is not an end unto itself. It should be part of the living processes of the project and is connected to progress tracking, standards, and analysis.

Build your project plan at a level suitable to the project needs. Use both top-down and bottom-up estimating to quality check your work estimates.

Chapter 7: It's Not What You Think It Is
Chapter Summary
While a project's objective may indicate a particular area to be the most important part of project success, a project leader understands the value of other areas.

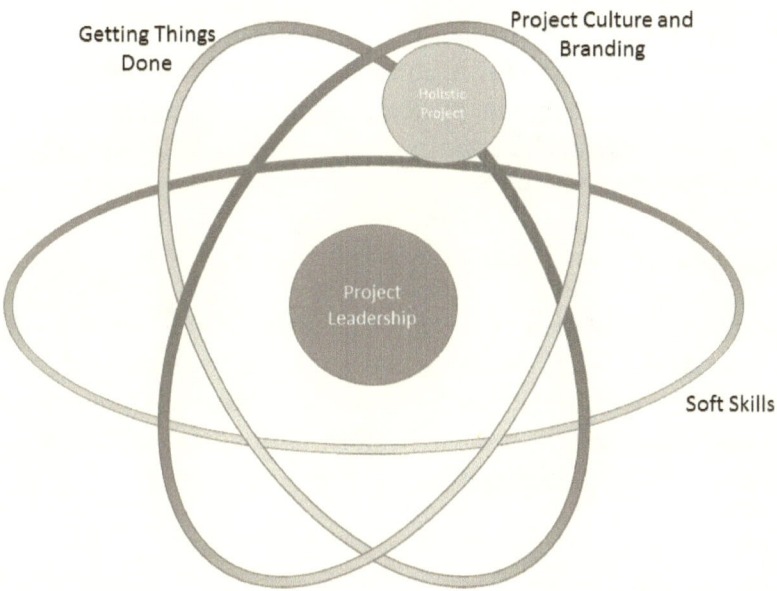

What Am I Missing?

Imagine you're working on a process project, documenting the process flow for a strategic business function. It looks and smells like a process project, right up until you realize you can't finish the process because you don't know what technology will be used to support it.

Or: Imagine you're delivering a new computer system, implementing a packaged solution with some customizations. This is obviously a technical project, but the system doesn't get any adoption because the training and communication hasn't been effective.

What's going on there? What were you missing?

The problem is that there's more to the project than our focus area. Sometimes what doesn't work is the stuff you didn't focus on. You do the core work, and it's beautiful, but the whole thing comes to a halt because of something that nobody knew was important, or that nobody knew how to do.

The Holistic Project

Blinding flash of the obvious, you say. Of course we could get tripped up on something we didn't anticipate! That's why we arrange complete coverage and plan everything out. There won't be anything we didn't plan for. We understand that success requires all of these diverse activities to be complete.

What often happens on a project, however, is not that we forget to take care of something, but that we lose track of how important that something is to ultimate project success. We might be able to finish the project without the missing ingredient. It just won't be as successful as it could be.

There are plenty of models for projects and solutions and their components. A classic is people, process, and technology, with "people" broadly reflecting training and communication. Too often we pigeon-hole our project into one of those broad classifications, and that becomes our focus. Yes, we did training and process work on our technology project, but it was the system delivery we were really worried about. Yes, we did a technical architecture assessment while we looked for process improvements, but we didn't really dig into it; we saw the process as being technology-agnostic.

Everyone's got a story about a technical project that was brilliantly delivered but was ultimately a failure because the users never liked the system.

The number one point here is that success really comes when every classification is taken care of, and everything is properly considered in the scoping and achievement of the project outcome.

Let me give you an example.

I was working on a project in Las Vegas with a chain of casinos (I mentioned this project elsewhere, in case that sounds familiar). We were implementing a packaged ERP system: purchasing, inventory, accounts payable, asset management, and general ledger. Sounds like a technical project then, right?

Not so fast. At the same time, we were instituting a shared services model, where multiple casinos under the same ownership would share an accounting and purchasing department, all of it powered by the ERP we were implementing. That sure sounds like organizational change management, doesn't it?

Oh, and we were also doing a strategic sourcing project at the same time, establishing a process for strategic sourcing in the company and using the process on a number of pilot products. Must be a process project then, huh?

It was all of them. And guess what failed? I can't even classify it properly. Maybe you'd call it process design. Anyhow, what broke the system eventually was reality.

You see, a casino isn't just a gambling hall. It's also a hotel, multiple restaurants, and possibly other retail operations. Some casinos are also zoos, theaters, amusement parks, or museums. Each of those business types has its own business requirements.

It was restaurants that broke our system. A Las Vegas casino on the Strip usually has some pretty pricey restaurants. Alcohol especially, but other food items as well, can be a big ticket item. So, to manage this effectively, we were asked to implement the inventory system for the restaurants.

I'm not a restaurant business process expert, so I'm not sure about the wisdom there. If I'm running a burger joint, would I separately track my inventory of hamburger patties or bags of frozen fries? Actually, I suppose I might, although I might try to find a unit of hamburgers larger than a single patty. You need to know when you're running out of things, after all, and what you need to order. So, sure, a restaurant ought to have an inventory system.

Here's where reality came in. What's one of the notable things about a Las Vegas casino? That's right: it never closes. Most of its shops never close, and many of its restaurants don't. When we turned on the system, it worked fine except for one thing. The system just couldn't keep up with restaurant inventory that was being constantly updated. Shipments of food and alcohol were showing up at every hour of the day or night. Items were being checked out of inventory twenty-four hours a day.

And because of system speed or the way the inventory stored process was designed, it could never catch up to what was actually in inventory at any given time.

People problem? Doesn't sound like it. Process problem? Maybe, only we got the process *right*. Why should we have suggested changing the process to account for the system performance? Technology problem? Yes, also maybe, since the system wasn't delivering the outcome we wanted. But again, the system did what it was supposed to do. It just couldn't do it fast enough to give good results.

In project management terms, that's what is called a non-functional requirement. It's not *what* the system is doing, it's the way in which it does it. Another example is system response time: when you load a new page on the website, the load time should be under X seconds.

Somebody probably wrote a non-functional requirement document for the system. It probably specified screen response times for each of the system modules. You know what? It might have even specified a requirement for how frequently or how quickly to process inventory. But we didn't focus on it. Nothing was done to satisfy that requirement, and I was running the system test, and we certainly never tested against it.

Consequence: project failure, followed by lots of investment to remediate the problem. I had moved on to another project long before this, so I don't know if the issue was ever resolved. My bet is they simply took the restaurant inventory out of the system and kept using their old tool.

The Weakest Link

The typical risk of a project not taking care of business is in the relative focus on people, process, and technology, as discussed in the previous section. There's another risk, too: the case where a chain of deliverables all need to be equally successful.

Most projects (even ones with iterative development) have dependencies: one task needs to be finished before another one can start. Usually that exists in the step by step completion of a deliverable. Sometimes, however, you get to a situation where multiple deliverables all have to be delivered, and if one of them fails, the others are worthless.

In a case like that, you can't treat any one of the links in the chain as more important than the others. You may be more worried about one than the others, but they all need to get delivered.

Another case study follows.

It was my first project as a manager. The overall project was modernizing the order entry and warehouse operations of a building supply company (aluminum siding, to be precise). At an earlier stage in the project, the client was suspicious that something was missing, but they weren't sure what.

This is a great example of raising one's hand to say that something isn't right. Don't keep pretending it's all going to work.

A two-week study was commissioned to investigate. A result was returned in two hours: there was a new order entry system going into production, and a warehouse management system to manage the picking and packing, but there was nothing to get the products on the truck. More specifically, there was no system for asking a truck to come to the warehouse.

That became my part of the project. We built a small custom system that would get information from the order entry system, knowing how much capacity was needed in a truck for the order, and then it would go out to trucking companies for bids for the load. This was all in the infancy of the internet and before the various forms of aggregators and consortia that sprang up a few years later. We had to do everything ourselves.

We eventually had a demonstration of the system for the client. It failed completely. I have to admit that, to this day, I have no idea what went wrong. We had a miserable night after this failure, but the next day our little part of the system worked fine.

Meanwhile, the warehouse management system was a catastrophe in the making. I'd heard that this particular packaged system had never worked, anywhere, and I was warned not to mention that to anyone. (That was somebody being a little less than candid with a client, by the way.)

Eventually go-live day came around and we turned everything on. I actually committed, on behalf of my team, that we would have two people on-site *at all times* during this stage. Twenty-four hours a day! I hope I never think of trying that again.

Anyway, what happened was that the order entry system worked about 90% of the time, the warehouse management system didn't work at all, and our little truck provisioning tool worked perfectly. So what do you think happens when you get 90% of your orders right but can't assemble a load, yet you still ask trucks to show up? That's right: you surround an aluminum siding factory with empty trucks.

This was not a successful project.

The client put up with this for about a week, then pulled the plug. So much for our system for provisioning trucks.

So what lessons did we get out of that?

On the plus side, the priorities were mostly in the right place. We were not being constantly badgered over the readiness of our provisioning tool, even after our demo had failed. You can probably imagine that, in a lot of cases, we'd have been getting the third degree about fixing our problems.

On the other hand, there were multiple negatives.

Project communication was all over the map. Because of my team's second-class citizen status, we mostly had no idea what was happening to the other teams. On one occasion the project director held a "come to Jesus" meeting with all of us in the open, furniture-free space on the second floor of the aluminum siding plant.

I remember it distinctly. There was Frank, the project director, yelling at a room full of people about the critical nature of the project. He had been in the Air Force, and he informed us that, from his Air Force experience, it was possible to get along quite well with only a few hours of sleep in any three-day period. This was not a motivating meeting.

It was also bewildering to my team, because as far as we knew, we were doing just fine. Why were we getting yelled at, they wanted to know. Did we need to do anything different? I did my best to calm everyone down.

The project was also sufficiently disjointed organizationally that there was nothing my project or I could have done to help the other parts of the project. Different providers were responsible for each piece, and we were mostly kept in the dark about what we were each doing. While there's nothing inherently bad about this arrangement, and it can even be good if you're getting specialist efforts in each area, it meant that there was no help around if there were issues.

Here's the second consequence from that: not only couldn't we help out when the warehouse management system failed, we weren't asked to provide any contingencies for what we could do. I recall being in a discussion about an entirely manual process for handling orders, but our suggestions were ignored. What this meant was that we were never asked to stop sending out requests for trucks, or to modify the approach to match up to what the other systems were doing. Our client had to pay for each of those trucks, whether they ever put anything on them or not.

A final lesson: sometimes you're only in charge of one piece of a larger initiative. If your part works fine, but everything else falls apart, was it a successful project?

I'd like to rate that one a success, and it was a huge growth experience for me as a manager. However, it sure doesn't sound like a successful outcome when the system was only up for a week and we filled a small town in Ohio with empty trucks.

Whac-a-Mole[5]

How do you manage a complex project? How can you tell what needs your attention, and how much attention to give it?

I think I'm not the only one who has drawn a parallel between project management and Whac-a-Mole. That's the arcade game where you have some sort of a mallet and moles pop out of the board and it's your job to whack them when they appear. A problem comes up, and you whack it. You hope you can whack it hard enough it never comes back, but that's not actually the way Whac-a-Mole works, I think.

It's not the way project leadership works, either.

I'd like to say that you'd get better results if you took care of the mole, nurturing it and making it a better contributor to society. Actually, I think we'd be better off ditching the mole analogy and trying something else.

If you're constantly bashing moles, you're not in charge of the priorities. You're always being reactive.

Come on, you may be saying. Sure, you can't tell where the next mole is going to pop up, but I can't tell you where the next fire on my project will flame up, either. Complete parallel. Whac-a-Mole analogy confirmed.

Constant vigilance!

Actually, here is where one of the most under-used project management tools comes in useful. Say hello to the risk register. Variously called the risk mitigation plan, risk log, and risk mitigation action plan (among other names), the risk

---

[5] Whac-a-Mole is the trademark of Bob's Space Racers, Ltd.

register is used to identify things that might happen. Usually the log includes a rating of the likelihood of each risk and the severity of impact should the risk occur.

In common usage, the risk log is assembled at the beginning of the project and then it sits, unchanged, for the life of the project. The risk log is brought out occasionally to demonstrate that the project has such an artifact, and then it is wheeled back to its lonely corner of the project document repository until the next audit.

Why does it receive such treatment? On the surface it seems to be such a useful document. Of course we should know what risks there are which could rise up and impact our project. We should be watching this like a hawk!

I think there are two reasons why the risk plan is so ignored. First, the risks logged are often not the risks you should be worried about. They're things like "Economic downturn hurts company's profitability" or "System integrator goes out of business". They tend to be distant and relatively unlikely.

Second, of all the classic project management documents, it has the least obvious actions related to it. You can have a weekly meeting to ask about issues, but risk lists tend not to change very often, so their weekly meeting gets tedious and soon abandoned. Most people are satisfied to complete the risk log and mitigation plan, secure in the knowledge that they have checked off a deliverable and now have a small insurance policy against risks. Oh, that risk? We've got a mitigation plan for that!

So there are two actions to make the risk log meaningful: document more specific risks and a more active plan to manage the risks.

Let's talk more about this and how they connect.

No one ever has a risk that says, "Project team fails to deliver". Some people would say that doesn't fit the definition of a risk, so they don't put it on the log. "Every other document we have is about ensuring our success," says the logic. "We don't need to document our own failure as a risk."

Here's why it should be on the list: your risk register should identify things which could impact the project achieving its business objectives, not just things which could impact the completion of a deliverable.

Does that make sense? The distinction here is that a project deliverable, like a process design or a computer system, is *not* the business outcome. It's something which enables the business outcome.

Don't confuse a deliverable with the project outcome.

When you look at it that way, it should become clear that a deliverable not being satisfactorily completed could endanger the project's success. You won't want to drown your risk log with risks for every single deliverable, but then, not every deliverable has an equal chance to torpedo your entire project.

Here's the next reason it should be on the list: while the risk register classically identifies mitigation plans for each risk (usually at the level of three sentences of business jargon), what you really need to be doing is building risk scenarios.

Think of risk scenarios like war games. If events A and B take place, what do we do next? If event C takes place and event D doesn't, what do we do?

The idea of scenario planning is not that you take actions regarding every scenario, any more than you actually execute a risk mitigation plan in advance of the risk occurring. Instead, you use the planning to assess the project's state of readiness. If you make an organizational change, maybe it supports scenarios 1 through 4, but not scenario 5, while a different organizational change supports all five scenarios.

In fact, you probably do something like this every time you consider a change.

Let's look at the truck provisioning example above for that. A reasonable scenario planning approach might have been to have examine the case where any one of the three components did not get delivered, the scenarios where two of three did not get delivered, and another where they all failed.

Here's the big shift in thinking: with a risk, the project manager looks at it and makes a brief statement about what would reduce the impact should the risk come to pass. Scenario planning is a much more in-your-face situation. So the warehouse management system might not work. *What are you going to do about it?*

The nature of scenario planning is that it tends to be a little higher level. You might have thirty items on your risk plan, but you couldn't give reasonable attention to thirty different scenarios. So, for example, how would this approach help in the restaurant inventory case we talked about earlier?

It's safe to assume that the specific issue wouldn't be noticed. We missed it as a test condition; it wouldn't have made it to a risk log, either. But if we identified scenarios around each of the system modules (e.g., purchasing, inventory, etc.), we should have easily arrived at "Inventory module fails to perform as expected". We might not have been able to predict all of the multitudinous reasons that could have happened, but we would have been in a better position to react when the problem showed up.

Another way the scenario planning can help out is in reviewing the scope, schedule, and budget. Management has told you that something needs to be trimmed, and your scenario planning will tell you what part of the project has the least impact.

The last piece of advice in taking the scenario approach and distributing your focus on the different parts of the project is to be consistent. Don't give your team whiplash by being freaked out by inventory one day and accounts payable the next. The point is to have visibility and monitor the challenges in every area. You might need to stress one area over another to keep it in line, but keep the overall priorities consistent from day to day and week to week.

This sort of steady, controlled approach will continuously build confidence with your team and stakeholders and keep the team heading for success.

Chapter Wrap-up

When there is too much of a focus on one dimension of a project, it is likely to fail because of another dimension that has not received appropriate attention.

A project is successful when all parts of it are successful.

A project's own progress and achievement of its objectives should be tracked as a risk.

Chapter 8: What to Do When Things Go Wrong

Chapter Summary

Project leadership identifies projects in desperate situations, determines if it's worth rescuing them, and understands the extraordinary means necessary to get a project back on track.

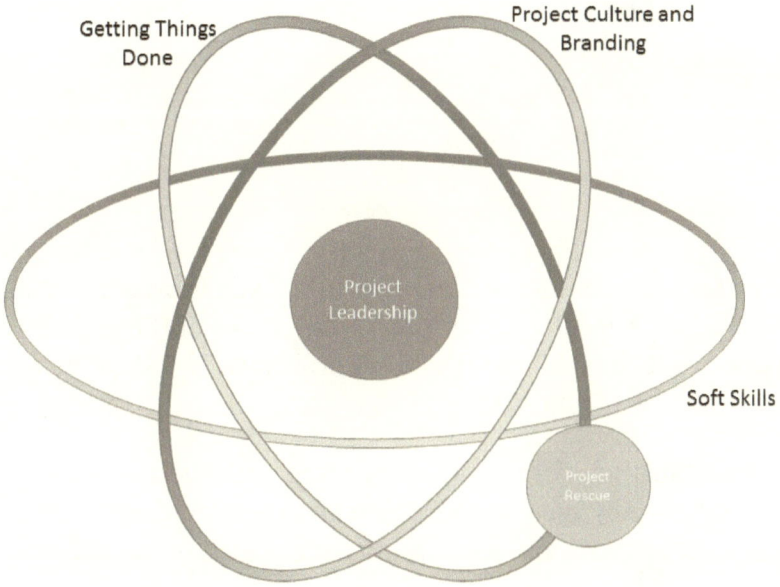

How to Tell a Project Needs Rescuing

I've seen various statistics over the years of the success rate of software implementation projects. One report had the following statistics based on the methodology used by projects from 2002-2010:

	Waterfall	Agile
Successful	14%	42%
Challenged	57%	49%
Failed	29%	9%

The metrics are usually used to point to the superiority of Agile over Waterfall, but I get something different out of these numbers. I get that 86% of Waterfall projects and 58% of Agile projects fail or are "challenged".

There are plenty of other studies out there with their own figures, but the key message is this: well over half of software development projects will face "challenges" - at the very least.

Obviously, you'll want your projects not to be in that list. And let's generously say that your projects never have those sort of problems. But other people's projects do, and sometimes someone comes along and drafts you to rescue their project.

Rescuing projects is plainly a common activity. Too many projects need help. This is intensified because so few projects simply get killed when they have problems.

Sometimes there's a misunderstanding of the level of difficulties which may be faced, and project sponsors think a project is close to being pulled out of the fire when, in fact, it is completely ablaze.

Sometimes the answer is to adjust the project's goals, sweep some issues under the rug, declare victory and pretend that this is where you were headed all along. That's not being dishonest: that's being honest about how the project value measures against continued investment.

And sometimes there's a feeling of stubbornness, not unlike the primary participants in World War I: after all the effort and cost, the only justification for the sacrifice is victory.

An early question is the extent of the problem you're facing. A project may be facing challenges, but they're surmountable challenges. The core activity of the project can be maintained, the objective remains the same, but other changes are needed. The schedule should be re-baselined, perhaps, the team structure modified, and maybe a few adds, changes, and deletes on the team roster.

In some companies, some proportion of projects are expected, and perhaps even desired, to fail. There may be a spirit of, "If we never fail, we're not pushing the envelope enough." At Microsoft (at least at one time), there was a philosophy of permitting multiple competing projects to operate, with the best one surviving. If you're in an environment like this, there's probably a protocol for handling the projects that aren't going to make the cut. A desperate rescue attempt would be a waste of time.

Lastly, there are the projects that truly in desperate shape. How can you tell if your project is one of these?

The less emotional way to judge a project is by what the risks are compared to where the project is in lifecycle.

Early in the project, an indication that a rescue may be needed is that the project has significant issues that are already indicated as "red", with near certain impacts on schedule, although no delivery dates may have been missed yet.

In the middle phase of a project, danger is suggested by significant issues indicated as "red", preliminary delivery dates have been missed, and it is becoming apparent that deployment dates cannot be met.

Late in the project - near when the project should be completing its deliverables - the need for rescue should be obvious: the project has missed delivery or deployment dates, and not by a week or two.

Those are the unemotional answers. However, if you're using words like "rescue", you've probably got a pretty emotional situation.

That sort of situation looks like this:

The project is in dire straits. It cannot practically achieve its objective, schedule, or budget. Stakeholders question the value of the project. Projected benefits are openly ridiculed. People associated with the project cannot agree on the situation, and rarely agree with each other on anything else.

Even a straightforward declaration on meteorological conditions will be challenged.

In short, something has gone terribly wrong, and incremental change will not work. The project is drowning and needs to be rescued.

Given the dreadful situation the project finds itself in, it should be no surprise that the remedy will be uncomfortable.

A project cannot be rescued without significant changes to its structure, scope, resources, approach, or objective. If all it took was a minor tweak, you wouldn't be talking about rescuing it.

So when we talk about rescuing a project, all of those things have to be on the table. If anything is kept off, you're restricting your ability to make the changes necessary for success.

Failure Is Always an Option
The next tough discussion:

Should this project be rescued? Maybe we should just kill it.

Too often, this gets answered with emotion rather than business or technical logic. The people who are likely having this conversation have bought into the project's value. They may have a personal stake in its success.

However, it's important that this question gets asked. You should anticipate that the rescue effort is going to be extraordinary. It's going to break rules. You will do things that may not follow a methodology or organization guidelines. The guard rails used to get the project approved and into the portfolio are going to be bent or simply driven around.

When we answer the question of whether the project should be rescued, we're also answering whether these extraordinary means are acceptable.

A project in "rescue" status should be forced to justify its continued existence, over and over.

The justification may be simply that the cost of the rescue is warranted and accepted, but it's just as likely that the explanation will be that there is simply no choice. Those are toughest justifications, because they're absolutes. Someone says, "Failure is not an option", and they expect the conversation to be over.

So, even with absolute requirements, there's still room for evaluation:

*   If the project is a requirement to compete in the
        marketplace, is there any other way to achieve the same
        requirement?

*   If the project is needed to achieve legal compliance,
        evaluate whether the entire project is needed for that.
        Is there a narrower solution which will satisfy
        requirements?

*   If the project is needed due to technical exigencies
        (enterprise software out of support window, for
        example), are there non-technical resolutions? Can
        support be purchased from a third party, for instance?

If no alternatives exist, or the benefit is still worth the pain,
then it's time to rescue the project.

The Rescue Operation

Normal completion of a project follows a standard set of steps to completion, and rescuing a project is no different. It's simply that the steps are a little unusual.

1. Face reality

2. Change the rules

3. Determine the problem you need to solve

4. Recast the project objective

5. Bite the bullet

6. Put it all in motion

The first step in conducting the rescue operation is facing reality.

Reality check #1: the project needs a whole lot of help. Tweaks and quick fixes aren't going to be enough.

Reality check #2: worry about reputation and blame later. No matter how you got in the hole, now you've got to get out of it.

Reality check #3: everything will be different until you get things sorted out. You'll change the rules, change the methodology, and ask people to take on things nobody planned. At the same time, the project will be under extraordinary scrutiny. As the project leader, you'll be spending a lot of time answering questions that seem rather personal. Your team will ask why nobody trusts them. The fact is, the entire team has to earn its trust back.

The next step: change the rules. If the rules had been working for you, you wouldn't be in this situation.

Rule change #1: no sacred cows. There is no requirement or objective that should be safe. Is your sponsor really willing to sink the entire project to keep alive some feature they fell in love with?

Rule change #2: get the right people doing the right work. Forget your project organization. Don't assume that anyone still has the same job, or any job at all. Everyone on the team has to be doing something needed to rescue the project; if not, they need to go away. Maybe they can be loaned to another team for a while, or maybe they're contractors who can be rolled off. Clear the decks!

Rule change #3: do only the work you need to. Don't worry - there should be plenty of it. The point is that you should ditch low-value-add work that distracts from the team's focus.

Rule change #4: open the communications channels. There's a good chance this project got where it is because people didn't share information. Take down the barriers. Anybody can talk to anybody.

Case in Point

One of the more memorable experiences in my career was being assigned to a project that was two months past its delivery date the day I walked in the door.

The situation was this:

The project was critical for delivering on contractual promises. A past project manager had also done a lot of the programming work, but he hadn't written anything down. All of the people on the project were former employees who were getting laid off, either because they were not considered critical in an organizational consolidation, or because they had declined the relocation package.

There were many other fun characteristics of the situation, but those were the ones pertinent to our current topic.

When I was brought in, it was framed mostly as a "drag this across the goal line" situation. It was November: if we could make some quick fixes and get something moderately acceptable by January or February, everyone would be happy. The whole mess could then be shut down and forgotten.

I tried pasting bandages over the wounds for three weeks until I came across a huge issue. I became convinced that the situation couldn't be saved. Then a business stakeholder came to the rescue, offering a critical solution which restored hope.

Three more weeks went by. I can't recall specifics, but I imagine I must have convinced myself that actual progress was being made. Then I found another huge issue.

The cavalry wasn't coming to the rescue this time. The project needed to be re-booted. It needed a new schedule, a new approach, and probably a new team.

To her credit, the director took this news as a constructive suggestion. She asked me to work out two plans: the re-boot and a "wrap this up and call it done" option.

I'd already seen enough to deeply hope a simple declaration of victory would suffice, but I knew there was no chance of that. I laid out the two plans, and the re-boot was approved.

As part of the plan, I made my recommendations for changes to the team roster. There was a person on the team who was of pretty low value at this point. I'd originally thought she had crucial information that we would need to rely on, and kept her on so far. If this was just a matter of getting us over a finish line, a replacement would take too much time. With a re-boot, however, she required far more effort to manage than was warranted by her contributions. I recommended we roll her off and replace her. Additional resources were also requested.

We made those changes, recalculated the budget, and away we went.

So what did I do right?

*   I had asked the question up front, "Can you just kill this project?"

*   I had had the courage to propose a re-boot, essentially a rescue operation.

*   I proposed changes to the approach, team organization, and resources.

Bully for me. So what did I do wrong?

*   I didn't go far enough with the changes. I was asked to develop a schedule for the re-boot, and I had done so,

even though no one would give it any support. I knew the schedule was a fiction: I should have said so, and said that we couldn't possible promise a due date.

* I didn't push the envelope on the project approach enough. I'm not a devotee of any particular methodology, but this was a classic example of the right place for an iterative methodology (i.e., Agile, Lean, Scrum). In combination with showing a backbone on the schedule, I should have insisted on changing to an iterative methodology to focus our work differently.

* Having established the first two points, I should have stood behind them and said that my continued leadership of the project was contingent on making those changes. Anything else, and I couldn't commit to any results.

* Lastly, I should have worked to build more support. If you're going to throw down an ultimatum, you ought to have people know what you're planning. As it happened, I stepped a number of people through my thinking and got assistance in the planning activities. What I didn't get was anybody sharing the burning platform with me.

That's another good lesson in project leadership: don't do it alone!

Rescuing the Project, Part 2

The next critical step in rescuing a project is determining what problem it is that you're trying to solve. Actually, you should probably have a pretty good idea of this at the reality check phase, but here's where you start getting down to brass tacks.

Leo Tolstoy is quoted (with variations based on translation) as saying, "All happy families resemble one another, each unhappy family is unhappy in its own way".

Restate that with successful projects and unsuccessful projects, and I think there's still a lot of wisdom there. You can certainly categorize the high-level issues that led to a project's rescue operations, but what you usually see is a web of issues. It's the combination of factors which brings about the uniqueness of the situation.

Still, there is likely to be one stand-out issue which has presented the largest barrier. Possible situations include:

*   Attempting the impossible

*   Using the wrong tool for the job

*   Doing the wrong work

"Attempting the impossible" can cover a large area. It's also an unpopular concept: visionaries and leaders are constantly trying to convince the rest of us that nothing is impossible, that we have to dare to dream, and that impossible simply means that no one's done it yet.

Far from being a criticism, our society glorifies those who attempt the impossible.

Consider some of these quotes:

"The difference between the impossible and the possible lies in a man's determination." (Tommy Lasorda)

"There is nothing impossible to him who will try." (Alexander the Great)

"Nothing is impossible. The word itself says 'I'm possible!'" (Audrey Hepburn)

"Everything is theoretically impossible, until is it done." (Robert A. Heinlein)

So we're all exhorted to attempt the impossible. We just don't always treat the failures very well, especially when they come up short on their cost-benefit analysis.

If you prefer, you can replace "impossible" with "not possible with finite resources" or "not possible with current conditions, resources, and constraints". This actually helps frame the problem better. Instead of saying, "It can't be done", it changes to "It can't be done without X". Once you've said that, you can discuss what *can* be done, or how to obtain X (more money, different technology, cooperation, etc.)

Then again, sometimes a project is designed to do something that just can't be done, in which case, the sooner the objective is changed to something achievable, the better.

A company I worked with a long time ago used Wang minicomputers for voice mail and electronic mail. This was before the internet, by the way. Somebody had the idea of connecting the voice mail to the email: you should be able to have your voice mail read your email to you, or use voice mail to create an email. Twenty-five years later, you can do these things with occasionally amusing results, but it's not the way most people access either messaging technology. The company was way ahead of its time and put considerable effort into doing this. Eventually, however, they wisely concluded that their resources were better spent elsewhere.

Similarly, Microsoft's Project Longhorn had visionary ideas for how to reinvent the personal computer operating system. Limitations of available technology eventually forced a retrenching and the delivery of Microsoft Vista: it was a considerable improvement over its predecessor, but not the revolution that had been planned.

Sometimes it's wise to accept what can be done and build on that.

Using the wrong tool for the job is a common problem. My example earlier in this book about making SharePoint work like Facebook is a case in point.

Sometimes switching to the right tool can be a simple activity. I had a summer job a million years ago in the real estate department of a big company, and it was my job to automate the creation of check requests for paying the rent on the company's sales locations. I used a word processor with mail merge to accomplish this. This was a start, but it was sub-optimal. The word processor didn't share information with anything else, so it was barely a step up from a manual activity. It made the check requests look nice, and they printed faster.

My successor redid the whole thing using an early PC database program. It not only created the form, it was better at managing the data it was using.

Not a major revolution to make that change.

Sometimes, however, changing tools means major upheaval. Upheaval, that is, at the level of throwing out all the work that has already been done.

That's where real project leadership comes in. How do you make that case? How do find a way to salvage some of the investment?

The last category is that sometimes you're just doing the wrong work. This usually comes from cases where the objective itself is not quite in alignment with the actual business need. If the goal you're trying to reach isn't useful to the business, no amount of work is ever going to get you somewhere useful.

Having asked these questions and identified the major issues you're dealing with, then you're in a position to figure out what to solve. Does the team need to be reorganized? Does the architecture need to be revisited? In a typical "unhappy family" situation, you'll end up with five to ten different issues to deal with, which you then need to sort through to create a plan.

A common and reasonable next step in project rescue is to recast the project objective. In essence, move the goal posts closer to your kicker.

At this point, you've done a reality check to uncover the poor assumptions that were made. You've changed the rules of engagement to streamline your team and focus on the rescue activity. You've pinpointed the pain areas that need to be fixed to get the project back on track.

With all of this information in hand, you are now in a position to determine what the project can actually accomplish.

Maybe the scope needs to be smaller.

Maybe a different architecture is needed.

Maybe the new objective is more subtle. If the project was aimed at delivering a technical capability rather than providing a specific service, it may be that there's a solution of alignment. What I mean by that is, if you ask the question of what the end result needs to look like, you may find a different way to get there.

Case in Point, Part 2

Let me give you an example of how you can be out of alignment.

The US Mail (properly, the United States Postal Service), along with most postal services, has an interesting business model. It is a quasi-government institution, which results in it being a near-monopoly of certain services.

It's also a prototype of mis-alignment in serving the customer.

Answer these two questions:

1.   How does the US Postal Service make money?

2.   As a consumer, what service does the USPS provide?

Not the same answer, is it? The USPS makes it money by selling you things: shipping supplies, post office boxes, and insurance on shipping, but mostly it sells postage. For everything that's not bulk mail or parcels, this historically meant stamps. The moment you buy a stamp, the USPS has made money.

But as a consumer, unless you're collecting stamps, the value of the USPS comes in the fact that it will pick up a piece of mail from a designated location and deliver it to another (assuming you've attached adequate postage to it). The Postal Service's speed and effectiveness may be open to question, but ultimately, you care that the piece of mail you drop in a mailbox actually gets to its destination.

The USPS does not make money from delivering mail. (Okay, for business reply mail, every piece delivered has to get paid for, but let's focus on stamps here.) Delivering mail costs them money.

If they could sell stamps without delivering any mail, they would probably be very happy. It just so happens that most of us will only buy stamps if we have something to mail, so they keep doing the delivery part of their job in order to keep the stamp sales going.

What this means is that the service provider and the customer are not in alignment. What the service provider is selling and what the customer is buying are not the same. It's hard to deliver quality customer service when that's the case.

Virtually every other form of currency replacement suffers from the same problem.

So how does that connect back to what we were just talking about?

Well, imagine you're working with the USPS and you've got a project to help the service's bad financial situation. Actually, this just happened in 2014, and the proposed solution was: deliver mail less frequently. This reduces the cost while presumably keeping the revenue the same.

This proposal got slapped down for a variety of reasons, but a reasonable possibility if this had been implemented was that people would have actually reduced the mail they sent. This volume is declining all the time, but this change might have precipitated a bigger slide.

Even worse, it could open up the discussion to all sorts of ideas. If the US Mail is going to outsource delivery in some areas to UPS or FedEx, why not revisit everything about the business? Why does the USPS have a near-monopoly on mail delivery? The US Constitution only says that Congress has to provide for mail delivery; it doesn't say the government has to do it itself. This puts everything on the table, and pretty soon, maybe there's no US Postal Service. Probably not what anyone had in mind when the project started.

The problem there is the alignment. When you define the problem as "fix the fact that we're losing billions of dollars a year", the focus becomes the finances. As the cost and revenues are more separated in mail delivery than in a lot of businesses, easy solutions like reducing delivery spring to mind quickly.

So what was the correct business problem to solve?

There's no shortage of ways to restate the situation, but let's try this one:

"Transform the USPS into a stable organization which satisfies its obligations to the US government and maintains relevance to the consumer."

Maybe you could play around with that and set some other objectives around consumer market share. Maybe you could also inject something in there about the USPS employees, who were probably more up in arms about a reduced delivery schedule than the consumers.

Anyway, that's a start to things. If you set this more holistic objective as your goal, you realize that the solution has to be more comprehensive. Simply raising the cost of first class mail or reducing the number of days when mail is delivered just doesn't answer to the stability or relevance of the objective. There was also the proposal, years ago, to tax emails for the benefit of the USPS, under the premise that these emails replaced first class mail and were undermining the service's monopoly. Thankfully for progress, this idea was buried.

That said, let's spend a little more time here as a project leader in rescue mode.

A key challenge with finding an answer for the USPS is that there are some major assumptions here. To begin with:

*   Frequent (i.e., daily except Sunday) delivery to homes and businesses is the standard.

*   The USPS must deliver all types of mail, and is in fact the primary, near-monopolistic carrier for certain categories of mail. This implies an obligation to deliver mail of these types.

*   The USPS charges by the piece for mail delivered, following standard, published tariffs and international agreements.

*   The USPS must exist.

I'm not trying to make a political point that the Postal Service should be closed down. It's simply that, as a project leader, this is the sort of question you should ask.

Think of what doors open up when you challenge these assumptions.

Maybe you don't have home delivery every day but Sunday. We used to have deliveries multiple times per day in major cities, and we scaled that back. What's sacred about six-day a week delivery?

Maybe we outsource Saturday delivery to someone else. This isn't outrageous: in remote parts of Texas, for example, standard mail delivery is done by UPS (that is, the United Parcel Service - the brown trucks).

Maybe there's a kind of mail the USPS shouldn't bother with anymore. What costs the most to handle? Where are the biggest margins? If you were running a business, you'd be asking those questions.

What if there's another way to charge? How about a mailbox tax? You pay a tax just for the privilege of getting mail delivered to you. What if you could send all the first-class mail you wanted at no charge, as long as you had a mailbox license?

Some of these ideas were actually discussed during the recent Post Office crisis. The closure or consolidation of post office locations was considered, for example. Besides these more radical ideas, the USPS also added Sunday package delivery, examined innovative business areas, and reduced costs through processing center consolidation.

The point here is that during a rescue operation, everything has to be open for discussion.

Rescuing a Project, Part 3

Having recast the project objective and developed a new plan of attack, next comes the really hard part: biting the bullet and making the necessary changes to the project.

Up to this point in a rescue effort, pretty much everything has been academic in an MBA case study sort of way. It can be intellectually stimulating and even kind of fun.

Now, however, you have to organize and communicate all of the actual changes being made to the project, which probably include (at the very least):

*   Adding and subtracting project personnel, always with an eye towards rebuilding a cohesive, high-performing project team

*   Reorganizing the project team, including change of reporting responsibilities, change of job assignments, and an adjustment to work focus

*   Re-orienting and re-energizing the team towards the new objective

*   Starting to manage to a new work plan with new deliverables

*   Modifying project governance and control processes, including communication and strategic direction

*   Numerous detailed and logistical changes, such as for meetings (eliminating old recurring meetings and creating new ones), geography (reassigning team work spaces, modifying off-site meetings, or changing virtual work arrangements), daily schedule (limiting or enabling flexible work arrangements), and the like

*   Planning shifts to new tools, layout, or architecture

The common thread here is the communication with the team, and here is where the project leader is so important. The team, being presumably made of human beings, has got into a comfort zone, even if that zone has a lot of pain associated with it. They won't like change, and you're bringing in a potentially lethal dose of it.

The communication of this change will depend largely on the project's personality and the specific conditions the project is facing. Also, while you may have done a lot of the rescue planning behind closed doors with stakeholders, shielding most of the rank and file from the chaos, once you're ready to implement the plan, the closer you can be to full disclosure, the better.

The team needs to know what problems you're trying to solve, where the goal posts have done, and where they stand.

You probably can't promise anybody that their job is safe, but you can tell them what approach has been approved and what the new timeline looks like. You can tell them what changes will be permanent and what are hoped to be temporary. You can thank them for the successes achieved, and thank them in advance for their commitment.

Some of the trickier communications will be one-on-one. We've discussed project challenges in generalities, and per our expert in project leadership, Leo Tolstoy, we recognize that the issues facing any unhappy project are probably numerous and complex. It would be surprising to me, however, if there were no changes to the roles certain team members were playing.

It would be especially surprising if none of those changes had to do with changing an assignment based on skills and ability.

It's probable that you'll have someone who's valuable to the project, with lots of background knowledge and useful contacts, but who has been playing a role that they're not well suited for.

It's always a challenge to reduce someone's role while pretending they didn't just get demoted.

Frankly, I think it works best to assume they'll notice this development. Stress the value they still bring to the project. Encourage them to take the lessons learned and build towards their next opportunity to fill that role. Remind them how everyone's critical in the project's current condition.

With all the tough messages delivered, the new objectives up on the bulletin board, and a new plan in place, it's time to wind up the new toy and let it go.

From here, it can look a lot like operating the project in "normal" mode. However, you still have to remember that this is a rescue operation, and there are some special questions which you'll have to answer.

First: to tweak or not to tweak?

You've kicked off your new approach and four weeks have gone by. You're not seeing the progress you thought you would. You want to change something, but you're afraid of jumping in too soon, maybe creating whiplash for your team as they can't keep up with the pace of change.

There's no hard and fast answer to this, but I would lean to the side of continuous improvement here rather than fixedly staying the course. You should be more afraid of freezing in the headlights than of disturbing your team with tweaks.

Second: do we need to rescue the operation all over again?

The sad reality is that sometimes the rescue operation has to be rescued. Maybe the first approach wasn't the right one or conditions changed to thwart it. Maybe the operation accomplished some of its goals, setting the stage for another attempt.

As mentioned with the tweaking question, there's a fine line between staying the course and twitching every time a fly goes by. You'll be more aware of the conditions of a failing project, since you just went through that, and struggling with whether to re-boot all over again, or let it play out.

The discussion on whether to mount a new rescue operation should follow the same model as it did the first time. What will be different is that more time has passed and more money spent, and the project is still proving to be a tough nut to crack. Because of that, you'll want to take an even harder look at whether the project really needs to be done.

Third: do we need to rescue the rescuers?

Some of your team members may be full-time employees and permanently assigned to the activities of the project. Some may be contractors brought in to fill a specific temporary role. Some may be longer term contractors or consultants.

It's tempting to see your longest-tenured team members as some of your most valued resources. They've seen it all, they've discussed all of the questions about how to deliver the project, and they have a thorough grounding in the project's history, business need, and benefits. They're probably also critical to the project's personality.

Sometimes, though, it's time for them to move on.

The project might need a fresh perspective, which they are unable to provide.

They may be resistant to adjusting to the project's new objective. It might be subtle: they might say the right things and seem to do the right work, but then you'll hear things like, "Well, if we were using the old tool," or "We already solved this problem". This may be undermining the rescue.

If you foresee some of this behavior, you would want to talk to them and get their perspective. Are they going to be able to make the mental transition that's necessary? Do they support the new objective whole-heartedly? Or do you just sense fatigue, and someone who has had their fill of the project?

Even if the person's knowledge and skills could be valuable to the rescue operation, a project leader has to make the call on whether they'll be a net positive for the project if they stay on.

Fourth: when is it not a rescue operation anymore?

From the positive side, if all goes well, you'll cruise through the challenges, get into a new rhythm, and be on course to deliver your project's objectives. At this point, it may be tempting to take your foot of the gas pedal. Those rules demanding everybody be at the project site from 9 to 5 every day? Maybe we can let them slide. The daily status calls at eight in the morning? Maybe we don't need them every day. Those weekly discussions with the CIO? Maybe we don't need his help so much anymore.

I'd like to be able to say that it's okay to ease up, and that there's a simple set of criteria for when you can do that.

Not going to do that.

It will always be a rescue project.

Your stakeholders will always have some doubt. Your team will always be nervous and touchy when they see the steering committee meeting longer than normal.

If you were in charge of the project when the need for a rescue became apparent, you'll always be trying to win back confidence from your management. If you were brought in to save the day, they'll wonder if you're only good at firefighting, and whether you can manage a project day to day.

The process of earning back trust takes longer than the life of most projects.

It may be that you can reach the project's objectives and do a reset for the next phase, but until you've hit the objectives, you're still rescuing the project.

Chapter Wrap-up

Rescuing projects is also a function of project leadership. Key activities in project rescue include:

1.   Face reality

2.   Change the rules

3.   Determine the problem you need to solve

4.   Recast the project objective

5.   Bite the bullet

6.   Put it all in motion

Soft Skills

Chapter 9: Life Lessons and Personal Models

Chapter Summary

We learn from experience, but to do so, we need to establish a personal model of behavior and goals that can help us make use of our experiences.

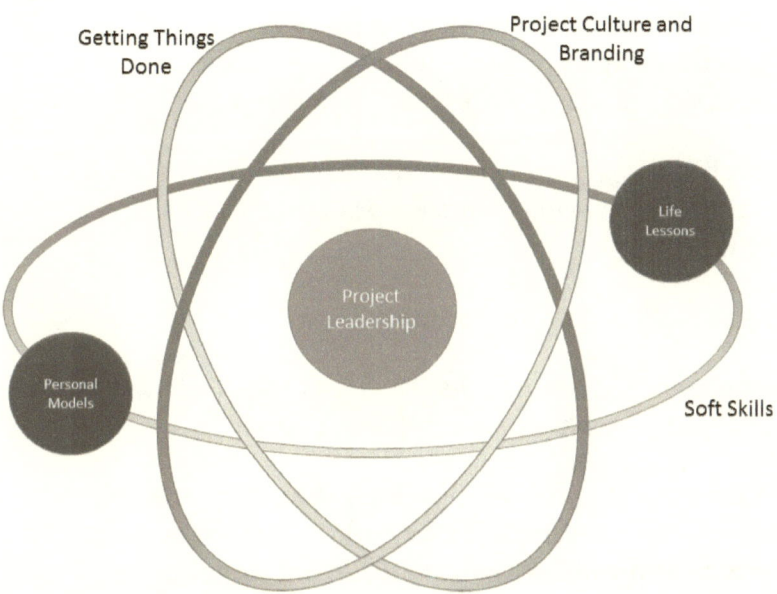

How We Learn

In previous chapters we've discussed the ways and means of the project activities. Experience with these activities can help you the next time around. So what's the best way to absorb these experiences and make them part of our knowledge bank?

Psychologists have compared a number of ways in which we learn. Rote memorization, highlighting, re-reading, skill practice, and cramming are all examples. However, these are skills applicable specifically to taking a classroom test, which is not a situation adults typically find themselves in.

More applicable for your career is learning by teaching and by doing. However, learning from experience isn't a passive activity.

Think about Mark Twain's example regarding a cat:

"If a cat sits on a hot stove, that cat won't sit on a hot stove again. That cat won't sit on a cold stove either."

The point is that the cat is just taking the experience -stove equals pain - and not applying any other analysis or insight to it. The cat got burned without noticing anything special about the stove. If the cat had noted anything useful - like a gas flame, a toasty feeling about the whiskers, or steam coming out of a kettle - and combined that with the experience of pain, then the cat would have gotten something useful out of the experience.

In short, we don't learn just by living. We have to think about our experiences, make sense of them, and turn the lessons into tools for handling future circumstances.

Here's an example of taking an experience and using it to build new habits.

Once upon a time, in the Paleolithic Age, I was at Consultant Boot Camp. Besides hand-writing code in COBOL, we had other sessions intended to prepare for us our future project roles. One of these was titled "Interviewing Skills". I don't think the hour we spent really taught us much about interviewing as a holistic activity, but I certainly learned a lot from it anyhow.

Here's what we had to do:

The class was split into pairs. In each team of two, the partners had identical sets of three dominoes. One person set up the three dominoes behind a screen in any fashion they chose. The other person asked questions, trying to learn how the other's dominoes were arranged and using their set to visually represent what they'd learned so far.

I was the interviewer. I completely failed. By the time the fifteen minutes were up, I was the only interviewer in the room who had not successfully determined his partner's arrangement of dominoes, and I was also completely frustrated. I don't know what my partner thought of the situation, but she probably thought I was some kind of an idiot.

So what happened?

My partner had set up her dominoes in a triangle, with the back two on their edges and the front one on its back. I'd gotten stuck when I asked two questions that involved which domino was touching with other one, and I couldn't understand how the domino on its back could be touching both of the others.

I had two problems here.

First, I had gotten stuck on the domino paradigm. In most forms of domino games, dominoes are either in line with each other or turned ninety degrees. I tend to arrange things at right angles anyway, but with dominoes, *of course* they had to be at right angles to each other. It absolutely never occurred to me that my partner would arrange them in a triangle. My partner, however, had never played dominoes, and so was not thinking in the domino paradigm at all.

Second, and by far more problematic, was that I had misinterpreted the exercise. I'm a very analytical person, and I had immediately jumped to the conclusion that this was a sort of "twenty questions" exercise. The problem with that model is that it's adversarial, but the exercise was not at all intended to be so.

In fact, the person who set up the dominoes wanted me to get it right. She wasn't trying to hide anything, and it was my fault for asking poor questions.

I've since concluded that the correct first question is, "Tell me how the dominoes are arranged." You ask the open-ended question, gather information, and then get more specific if you didn't get the understanding quite right.

Seek first to understand (thank you, Mr. Covey).

I've learned a whole tool chest of lessons from this.

First, usually, when you're asking for an explanation, the person you're talking to *wants* you to understand. You're not cross-examining witnesses. You should be letting yourself be educated and persuaded.

Second, paradigms are deadly. Even with my poor interviewing strategy, I might have saved the day if I wasn't trapped in my right-angle domino metaphor.

Lastly, both of the first two lessons are highly applicable to real life situations. This wasn't just failing at a party game. There have been literally hundreds of times since when I've had a similar sort of interviewing circumstance, trying to learn from a client or teammate. I've had plenty of other cases I've observed where the set of possible solutions was constrained because of a base assumption.

To take lessons from an experience like this and turn them into tools for the future, we need a structure in which to fit our experiences, and then the time to break down what happened. In this chapter, we'll start by talking about structures, then move on to examples.

Behavior Paradigms

There are plenty of different models for professional behavior. When I say "model", I mean a construct of principles that you can follow and assess your experiences by.

It's critical to consider these from the perspective of behavior. Ultimately, project leadership is about habit and character, and these are demonstrated through your everyday actions.

A common and very popular model comes from Stephen Covey.[6] It was so popular it spawned a partnership with a journal and notebook company (Franklin Planner). I never joined the hordes with their Franklin Covey personal journals, but I still often remind myself and others to "Seek first to understand" and "Begin with the end in mind".

They may seem like blinding of flashes of the obvious, but Covey earned his money by putting them together simply and powerfully.

You can create your own model, too. It might seem like a variation on Covey or some other best-selling paradigm, but you should feel free to make it your own.

At one time I considered what I really enjoyed about my work. I listed the key categories of activities I got from that. I found that it was important to me to exercise my creativity. I received strong emotional affirmation from contributing to my team's objective. Lastly, communicating with others was important: creating bonds with others, sharing ideas, and coaching and mentoring.

---

[6] Stephen R. Covey, "The Seven Habits of Highly Effective People", 1989.

I created my person "Three C's" mode: create, contribute, and communicate. If I was doing things in all three areas, it was a good sign for me. That became my own behavior model.

Finding Your Own Priorities

I concluded during one stage of my career that you usually have 24 hours a day of work to do, if you want it.

Your obvious project work might not be that much on any given day. Besides that, however, there might be personal development activities (reading blogs or magazine articles, researching technology and innovations, and so on). There might be coaching and mentoring of associates, perhaps including people not on your project. There might be other activities associated with your personal brand, such as social media, blogging, or preparing papers for seminars or professional societies.

How can you tell what to do?

Cast yourself back to being in college. You're a sophomore, and maybe it's Wednesday night and you don't have classes on Thursday. You're conscientious, so you don't immediately leap to the conclusion that now's the time for partying and staying up until three in the morning. You ask yourself, what else can I do?

If you're like most people, your objective while in college was to finish and get a degree. On our hypothetical Wednesday night, you can ask yourself if there's anything you can do which enables that goal. No, not today? Then let's get this party started!

The key there is that your objective was obvious. The problem so many of us face after college is that the goals are less plain. We have to pick them ourselves, and we can all come up with different ones.

So, with a full calendar day of work lying in front of you, and no obvious over-arching goal, what do you do? Stephen Covey has whole books on how you determine what's most important, but I think it can be summarized as follows:

It's up to you to decide how much of that work you need to do based on the goals you set for yourself.

If your goal is to be promoted, what do you have to do for that? Do you need to achieve a particular rating on your performance feedback? Do you need to contribute to the development of your company's intellectual capital?

If your goal is to establish certain elements of your personal brand, what will that take? What seminars or networking events do you need to attend? What papers do you need to get published?

Maybe your professional goal is static (such as maintaining your current job and the reputation you've built), but you have personal goals, like running a marathon, spending a certain amount of time with your family, or volunteering for charity events.

Logically, your personal rules for what to do will match up with the behavioral model you've worked out. Once you have identified your goals, you can check yourself against them constantly. It's up to you to set your priorities and work towards them.

Making Progress

One thing that is often missing from personal behavioral models is a sense of progress. It is assumed by the writer that any reader can make use of their information and adapt themselves to it. This seems reasonable, if only because the writer can't presume to anticipate every stage of development that a reader might experience. Neither can the writer project every possible personality quirk, previous experience, and the like that will modify their ability to make use of the recommendations.

Developmental readiness is a key part of learning and growing. We don't expect a four-year old to completely grasp social nuances, for example. Their mental readiness and life experience have to develop before they can adapt other instructions. This sort of thing is true at other stages, too.

Understanding how mental development connects to professional development is part of self-awareness in managing's one's progress. It is also key to coaching and mentoring.

Imagine a young person just out of college and taking on their first job. Or try to recall yourself at that stage.

That person has a limited understanding of the environment they're heading into. Internships or summer jobs may have given them a taste for how interpersonal business communication works, and what some of the expectations may be for their jobs. Still, an intern is never that much a part of the environment, and our new graduate may have been treated quite differently during that experience.

While an internship may have focused on a single project or a narrow responsibility, their new career is likely to be broader, with a greater demand on skills like flexibility, ability to manage one's time, and prioritization.

I recall a couple of the instructions I received early in my career that started to define expectations.

The first was the importance of speaking at a level of detail appropriate to the audience. We think of this generally as matching our message to our audience, but at an early stage in one's career, it basically means figuring out who to provide the boring details to. Your co-workers and your supervisor need the details; nobody else does. As you progress, there's very much an expectation of the ability to seamlessly transition one's style between someone more junior to you and someone in a higher position of authority.

Furthermore, one's ability becomes the indicator of whether one can operate at a higher level. In short, can you be promoted? If you always speak to the details, not to trends or guidelines that can be absorbed by an executive, you'll be seen as someone who can only operate at a low level.

Another principle I picked up was regarding candid communication. No one ever told me to lie. The point was that when I was speaking with someone from another team, I should not spill the beans on every problem we were facing. This is the sort of training we get to be cautious and guarded in a corporate environment, and by the time we gain more experience, we praise it in the sense of being able to "message effectively".

A third principle had to do with responsibility and hierarchy. It's abundantly clear from reading books and watching TV and movies that some people are bosses, while some people are being bossed. Since most people in the entertainment industry have never really worked in a "job", the business setting is frequently portrayed with serious stereotypes. There are the thoughtless (and clueless) bosses, for example. There's also the Machiavellian schemer. But there's also the simple idea that the bosses are the "big thinkers" who go to their clubs for three-martini lunches when the real work needs to be done.

One of the crystal clear moments in my own development came on a Saturday morning in the office. I was working with my manager to make print-outs of the presentation for the steering committee meeting on the following Monday. This sort of thing isn't a pleasant activity today, and it was worse back in those Paleolithic days. If I recall correctly, our printer had limited memory, which meant we could only print a few pages at a time or else the memory would overload and we'd have to reboot it.

So, our activity was to print the pages, sort them all out, and make sure we had enough copies. While the copies were intended to be distributed at the meeting, my manager also preserved one "master" copy. (By the way, this was also around the dawn of local area networks, so storing files on shared drive was a pretty uncommon thing. Important things got stored on paper.) While the distribution copies would be stapled, my manager would put a binder clip on the master copy so he could pull out selected pages for copying. Thinking ahead even beyond that, he put a piece of paper over the corner of the presentation so the binder clip would not mar the appearance of the first or last pages.

That sounds like a lot of effort, doesn't it? I realized two things, however.

First, this was simply giving the task the care that it required. It was doing the job right.

Second, it didn't matter that we were doing something that seemed terribly menial. It needed to be done, and it needed to be done right. When something needs to be done, it doesn't matter who does it. A leader will step in where they need to in order to get the job done.

There's one other item I learned although no one was able to put the principle into words. I recall being impressed that I'd be in some meeting and someone would make a good suggestion about what we should do next. A few years later, I'd be impressed when someone was able to speak confidently and off-the-cuff about the pros and cons of a particular plan.

It felt like I every time I suggested something, it got shot down. I didn't take it as a personal affront, but I did wonder why I never had an idea that was any good. Sometimes I'd have something that sounded like a good idea, but it would turn out someone else had already thought of it. And if I had an original idea, it would turn out to be absurd or inapplicable.

Eventually I figured it out. Ideas don't come from nowhere; they come from experience, significantly from the experience of discussing all kinds of ideas that weren't any good.

So, the first major career milestone:

You can have an idea that is both original and correct

Once you pass this milestone, you're really in a position to be able to contribute beyond being another set of arms and legs.

The challenge is getting to that point without having been scarred by rejection for all the ideas you had which were either unoriginal or wrong.

In the last few years I've identified a second significant career milestone:

You know how to define your own job

Think of a job. Any job. Any job you've been assigned to or hired into. You had an interview (probably). You were told what the circumstances were and (hopefully) what the expectations were. You might have been asked questions about what you did in a similar circumstance, but that was mostly to confirm your experience. It wasn't to ask you what you would actually do.

At nearly every role below that of the top dog in a department, building, or business unit, we almost never expect someone to walk in the door with a plan. The expectation is that the new person will fit in, taking on the plans, issues, and ideas of their predecessor.

Maybe you've been brought in because the person before you wasn't working out. In all likelihood, that's probably not because their ideas weren't any good. It was because they weren't executing, weren't meeting expectations. They weren't delivering results.

Achieving that second milestone is the hallmark of a project leader. This comes when you understand enough about the role, the environment, and the expectations that you can tell someone else - notably your boss or your client - just what the job is that you should be doing. It's what makes you different from your predecessor and begins your delivery of successful outcomes.

The person you're reporting to probably doesn't know everything that your job entails. Maybe they had a written job description for it. At the least, they've got experience of managing your predecessor, so they have an idea what the issues are. The fact is, however, that they don't know everything you'll have to do, or understand the priorities of the items on the job description. They may understand that you have to get a certain report in every week, but they may not realize what other processes that report enables. Maybe they don't realize that the report is actually a legal requirement, so you can't just skip a week if time runs short.

They need you to tell them what your job is.

It's also possible that your boss or client used to do the role that you're going to do. Maybe you've been brought in to replace them on their promotion. They've probably got a lot of their own immediate experience to share with you. "Item A determines your success." "Getting along with Person B is critical." And so on and so forth. You'll have to listen to them, absorb their experience, and fold it into your own plans. Then you come back with your own description of the role.

Their experience probably included things that don't need to be part of the job. For one thing, anybody's role usually has two parts: the items that logically fit the role, and then all the other random stuff that the person filling the role has collected over the years. They're still doing it because nobody could be found to pick it up. It doesn't mean those tasks really belong to that role, and by the time you come along, it's high time a new owner was found for it.

Once you've established that you're a good listener and appreciate the hardships your predecessor faced, your boss should appreciate your clarity in restating the role. What's critical, what's strategic, and what's going to have to get deferred until you hire someone else?

What does it mean to design your own role?

First, it means having independent expectations of your resources, not just accepting what you're handed. Your design should not just state a bunch of (unrelated) tasks and duties. It should connect them or justify why an outlier is included. It should also include the resources needed. That could be the skills and number of team members, or it could be facilities, technology, or access.

Second, it means defining the objective of the role. This doesn't mean you should be building a box around yourself. It means setting the strategic objective. What does success look like? What are the components which support it? How do you support those around you, and how does your work support the success of the whole?

Why define your own role?

Several reasons. First, you'll know better than anyone what the role should look like. You're living it, day after day. You're seeing what works, what doesn't, and what's a waste of time.

Next, it's empowering. It's taking ownership. It's easier to own the goals if you set them yourself.

It's also a positive contribution. It's not a passive acceptance of the way the world works. It's a take-charge approach to making a contribution.

Now, you may not always get the positive response you want from this.

Certainly, if you got hired to wash dishes, your boss is going to want you to wash dishes. He doesn't want you spending your time doing a time-motion study on dish washing, or conducting evaluations on dish soap quality.

In the project leadership world, however, defining your role is demonstrating that leadership. It's part of the personal brand you're trying to maintain. You may have to negotiate on the role, or phase in (or out) certain elements. You may even change your mind over time. No matter what, though, you should own the vision of your role.

Those are two pretty major milestones we've just discussed. First, going from newbie to contributor by being able to come up with ideas that are both new and original. Second, graduating to leadership by defining your own role.

I can see you, nodding with determination and positive energy, and you say, "This is great! Now, what's the third milestone?"

That's where you've got me. I don't know what the third milestone is yet.

But just as I've laid out the first two milestones from my own experience, you should be ready to look for the third for yourself. That's part of building your own behavioral model.

Chapter Wrap-up

Build your own personal model of behavior, reflecting your values, desired experiences, and desired outcomes.

An important early achievement of career maturity is being able to have an insight which is both original and correct.

An important later achievement of career maturity is being able to define your own effective role.

Chapter 10: Say It Now, Say It Loud
Chapter Summary
A project leader maintains positive, on-going communications in all directions, and fosters a project ethic of communications.

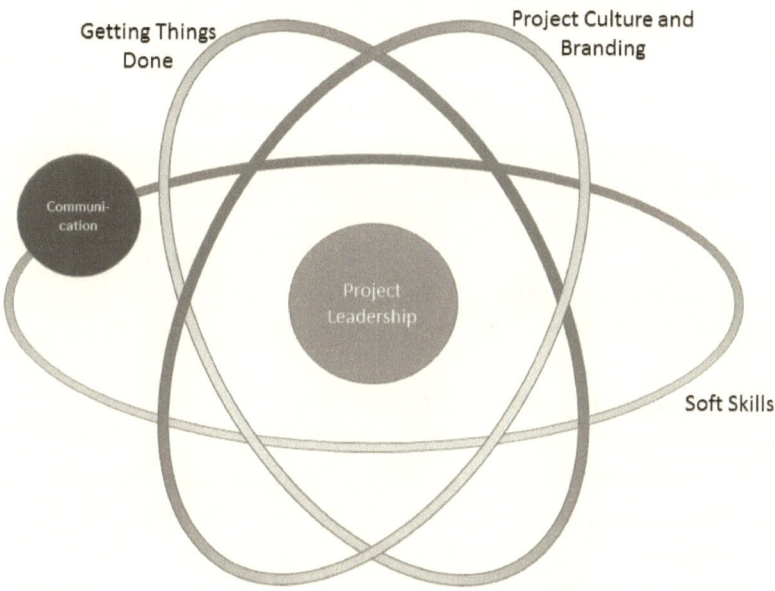

The Different Objectives of Communication

The ability of humans to communicate is often considered one of the things which differentiates us from other creatures. Because we sometimes see it as a tool we use unconsciously, we forget to pay attention to whether we're doing it well or not. We may also not be aware of how we're communicating.

Within a project or business context, there are a number of common types of communication. Here are some broad categories; while you're reading about them, think about each of them can be combined with the others.

* *Informing.* One person presents information for another's awareness. This includes project status, plans, and news regarding actions taken.

    This could be a one-way communication (such as an email), or it could be very interactive. Also, while we think of the person doing the informing as being the active party, in some cases the person who is being informed will have to drive the conversation. Imagine being a project manager trying to understand the issues confronting a team member. As a project leader, you are trying to understand the issue, its implications, and enough detail to frame future communications effectively. To do this, you have to ask questions to get to the information you need, as your team member may not understand how to present the information to you on their own. This may look more like an interview or a collaborative discussion.

* *Learning.* A person (or team) presents information to develop the skills or knowledge of others. This covers anything where someone is providing instruction with

an expectation that the person will then make use of the information to improve their contribution to the team.

As with Informing, this can take multiple forms. While in most cases it will be a simple one on one discussion, it could also be an open discussion, a structured classroom training session, or an interactive multimedia experience.

* *Collaborating.* A group of people is working together to solve a problem, create a deliverable or work product, or otherwise collectively contribute effort to a common goal.

  Some form of workshop might immediately come to mind, but this might also be something like pair programming, where two people work on project tasks in tandem, or some form of asynchronous communication such as jointly editing a document stored on-line.

* *Directing.* A person provides directions to one or more others, indicating a desired task to complete and the requirements of the task to be done.

  Note the potential similarity of the Directing and Learning communication objectives. You may often find yourself providing Learning communication right before Directing, so as to make the Directing communication more effective.

* *Bonding.* Multiple people on a team communicate in a way that builds team bonds. The communication may or may not have anything specifically to do with the project and its objective, but the nature of the communication helps build interdependence and

confidence among the team. In a particularly positive situation, bonding communication will take place at the same time as another type.

The point here is that every time you are communicating with your team, that probably fits into one of these categories. You want to be conscious of your objective and choose the setting, words, media, and tone that fit it best.

For example, sometimes you'll want to see how to combine communications to develop a generally positive and collaborative tone. As suggested above, you might find it effective to provide Learning right before Direction, or somehow combined with it, thinking of instructing your team member on expectations before they begin a task. You might also do that a different way: you might ask for Learning - that is, ask questions to understand a problem better - before shaping your Direction communication in the same discussion.

In another case, you might want the Learning to be clearly focused on the development of a particular skill (such as in instructor-led training) and may not want to confuse the message by including other types.

Another example: when you're delivering feedback to someone indicating that they're not meeting expectations, you probably won't want to do a multiple page presentation on the subject.

In short, be conscious of your objective. Know what you want to accomplish. Prepare for it with research, an agenda, or facilitation tools. If you're expecting action afterwards, wrap up the communication with clear next steps. Ask questions and look for other indications that the communications has been effective.

The Sub-Channel

The previous section was about conscious, intentional communication. You wanted certain information transmitted, received, created, or shared. You set a plan for it, and you made it happen.

Scientists say that a substantial part of our normal conversational communication is actually non-verbal. Your audience may actually get more information from how you say something than the actual words you use.

That's just in a single-shot setting of verbal communication. Now think about the context of a project. Every time you speak to someone on your team, it's in the context of potentially hundreds of other communications, not to mention the deep context of a shared enterprise and possible past relationships. They can hear what you say through a filter of many hours of past communications in diverse settings.

The message they receive will be significantly influenced by every message they've received from you before. Been evasive or unhelpful? They're still thinking about that. Been trustworthy before, and now you're making a withdrawal on that trust? Maybe you've got a chance.

Similarly, when you're communicating right now, you're setting the stage for future communications. Even if you're firing someone (or the one who's being fired), remember that it's a small world.

It's the tremendous depth of meaning potentially present in any communication that makes it so important to base your professional identity on character and good habits. TV shows and movies like to represent people in business (and corporate environments in general) as back-stabbing, Machiavellian settings where people do anything they can to get ahead. The fact is that it takes too much effort to be that complicated. It's all most people can do to actually get their work done without coming up with complex schemes to steal credit from their co-workers or discredit their boss. What's more, no one's good enough to cover their tracks if they did. You might pull off something like that once, but after that people know all about it.

So how do you send a message within a message?

* *360 degrees communication.* It's as important to communicate downward as upwards; and don't forget laterally, either. Some companies very much have a personality where people only want to communicate upwards so they can impress their boss. If that's what your team sees you do, it sends a message that they're not very important to you.

* *Make communication important - schedule it.* Communication within a team, or between team members, is always important. Prove it by putting it on the schedule. Set up time to meet one on one with your team members so you can hear their concerns and ideas. Not only do people like to be heard, you may see a number of other benefits from this less formal communication.

* *Make respectful choices.* How often have you had a meeting planned with your boss or your client, and had them cancel your discussion in order to have another one? How did that make you feel? While you might have accepted it happening once or twice, by the third time that happened, you probably felt like you weren't very important. That's not a trust-building event.

As a project leader, you won't always be able to avoid scheduling conflicts. It's what you do next that's important. Apologize. Don't assume this had no impact on the person you were supposed to meet with. Make it up to them by letting them set the time for the replacement. Show that their time is as valuable as yours.

*   *Make up your own mind; don't use somebody else's.* I'll touch on this more in the next chapter, but it fits here, too. Quite often you'll get advance warning about somebody you'll be working with. Maybe it's a team member who isn't a good performer. Maybe it's a thoughtless boss or a confused client. It might seem wise to use any intelligence like that to prepare yourself for a rough time of it.

    I'd agree with preparing yourself, but in a different way. Try to put yourself in their shoes. Think about how you can communicate with them to establish your own relationship with this person, rather than re-living someone else's.

*   *Don't avoid communication.* Work is hard. You've got a lot of it to do. What you don't need is having to deal with people you don't like or simply don't click with, right?

    The fact of the matter is, you don't get to be choosy about who you communicate with. If someone's connected to your project and its success, you're going to have to work with them. When you avoid someone, you lose all the benefits of communication. What's worse, they may notice that you're not talking to them. Are you hiding something? Does your avoidance mean something? Maybe they'll decide they shouldn't like you, either.

As a project leader, you should push yourself to seek out communication in a case like this. Try to learn more about the person. Make sure you listen to them. Make sure the lines of communication are open.

You may never want to invite them to your house for dinner, but you need to at least be on civil terms with them.

*   *Set expectations on communications.* When you join a project, you should establish expectations around communication.

For example, every time I start a project I discuss communications with my boss or primary stakeholder. Should we have a regular time to meet? How often do they want to receive communications from me? What form should our communications or interactions take? I'm not just trying to make it as clear as possible that communication is important to me. Every part of the message is that I will communicate in the way that meets their preferences. I want them to consciously set their expectations of our communications.

You can do that within a team, too. Do you expect team leads to meet with each of their team members regularly? How about with their whole team? How about the team leads together?

I'm not suggesting you flood everyone's work day with meetings. What you are trying to do is make sure the team understands the value of communication, and that you won't be really welcoming to project failures based on a lack of communication.

You'll often have situations where restrictions on communication may come up. A classic is where a manager or team lead wants to protect their team members from "walk-ups". They may ask all communications from outside their team to go through them. It may make all the sense in the world, and under some circumstances, it may be the right answer. However, I always try to establish the ground rule that anyone can talk to anyone else. Traditional channels may still be followed more often than not, but the sub-message is still valuable.

*   *Watch the non-verbal communication.* Things such as tone and posture are known issues with communications. Your words say one thing, your body says another. This is difficult to observe in oneself, but worth paying attention to. You might ask for feedback on this from someone you trust.

    Non-verbal or non-message communication can show up in other ways. Suppose you go to someone's desk to talk to them. You've asked them if they have a moment to talk, and they said yes. Now you're talking, but they're still looking at a computer screen or their phone. What message are you getting from that?

    Sometimes there's a sub-message in the words you use (what I just called non-message communication). That is, the sentence said one thing, but the words gave a secondary message. For example, you can say, "I really need that report on my desk by noon; is there anything you need to help make that happen?" Or you can say,

"Get that report on my desk by noon. I don't care what you have to do."

I recall a case a long time ago when the director of the IT department I was in spoke at an all-hands meeting. At one point he said, "Programmers don't bring anything to the party." What he *meant* was that we can hire lots of people just to be programmers, but we hire people as programmers with the expectation that they will develop, be promoted, and be part of a much larger success. We hire people for who they will become. That's not a bad message at all. The slangy expression he used, however, left the sense that programmers weren't valued at all.

Another sub-message lies in courtesy words. Does a person say "please" and "thank you"? It may sound unimportant, and often it is - right up until the moment you notice that a person never thanks you for anything.

I have a personal principle that the first thing I say to any person on a given day has to be unrelated to work. This is usually just "Good morning" and a sincerely intended "How are you?" I started this years ago after a day when I was at my desk at 7:30 in the morning, eating my breakfast, and my supervisor showed up and immediately started a discussion about some deliverable we were working on. There was nothing wrong with the discussion: we did need to work on it, and the tone was entirely pleasant and collegial. But there had been no recognition that I had been doing something else before he had arrived, and neither had he shown any courtesy with a simple greeting.

It's not just me. Say "please", "thank you", and "how are you" - and mean it - and watch how positively people respond to you.

* *Watch for what's left unsaid, or, don't draw attention to something by ignoring it.* Remember what I was saying about how much context people have to filter your communications? Here's a classic consequence: people notice when you're *not* saying something.

Imagine you've got a situation on your project. Someone's not being a good performer and there's been a lot of drama. It's starting to impact the team, as the gossip is overwhelming productive work. Will the person quit? Will they be fired or reassigned? You have a meeting to discuss project plans and you completely avoid the topic. You probably thought that you'd rather not distract the team with a topic that you really can't discuss with them, but now you've got even more questions to answer.

A favorite example of mine came during the early days of corporate portals and general internet use. The division I was in had just launched a portal, and somebody had the great idea of trying to create more dynamic and interactive content in the form of a survey. First question: what web sites do you visit most often?

What could be wrong with that?

Nothing. Yet.

Next week they publish the top ten web sites. Nine of the ten are shown in the list as hyperlinks; one of them isn't. It stands out like a sore thumb. So naturally I go to check it out. It turns out it's a web comic drawn by an employee of our company, making sarcastic comments about the work we do.

Now, I'm all for candor, openness, and honesty, but what was somebody thinking? Not the cartoonist - the person managing the portal. They clearly didn't want to draw any attention to this web site because they didn't want this subversion to be spread around. Fine, it's a company web site. So simply don't include it on the top ten list! Thinking that omitting its hyperlink would make it invisible was just silly. Instead it simply asked me to check it out, which I probably wouldn't have done if there had been a hyperlink for it.

* *The medium is the message.* Learn what tools people like to communicate with, and use them. Your stakeholders may use email, your teammates use the instant messaging tool which came installed on the company laptops, and your incredibly hip development team uses an esoteric web forum full of macros and in-jokes. You may want to set a project standard for some kinds of communication, if only to make sure that not every sub-team has its own and you can never find anybody online, but you need to recognize that the tools people use are part of their personal identity.

I remember being surprised years ago when members of my team wouldn't respond to voice mail (this was before ubiquitous email). It turns out some of them weren't even listening to it. They just didn't *do* voice mail. If you want people to respond to you, you have to send them a message they'll actually receive.

As with the different communication categories in the previous section, these secondary messages can also be combined.

Here's an example of how some of these can come together to have a significant impact on a project.

I had a project where I took over in the middle of things and had been thoroughly warned about the deviousness of my client. He would apparently promise to do one thing, then say something entirely contrary in a presentation. I also found he was tremendously busy, so getting his time was going to be difficult.

We ended up scheduling lunch together every day. Now, I normally see lunch (if I get to take it) as my little vacation in the middle of the day, and would rather not eat lunch with anybody, but I knew this was important, so I made the sacrifice. Every day I prepared an agenda: what did I want him to know, what actions did I need him to take, and what questions did I have for him.

We didn't eat lunch together absolutely every day, but we probably managed three days a week. The prepared communications kept him well-informed and got me his feedback every day. We also got to know each other personally much better.

One of the things I figured out from all this was that he wasn't devious or back-stabbing at all. He was just very busy. What had happened was that my predecessor had dumped too much information on the client. He'd forgotten some of it, so when he went into a presentation, some of the answers got made up on the spot.

Not only did realizing this help establish trust between us, it also gave me the knowledge I needed to help him deliver presentations. I reduced the number of points to cover and also had preparation meetings directly before the presentations. Never had a problem after that.

Chapter Wrap-up

You should be conscious of the objectives of your communications, sticking to those to stay focused and maintain clarity.

Broad categories of communications are Informing, Learning, Collaborating, Directing, and Bonding.

Secondary messages in communication need to support the primary messages. Focus on word choice, tone, body language, respectfulness as supporting cues.

Make on-going communication a part of your project's ethos.

Chapter 11: Coaching and Mentoring
Chapter Summary
Project leaders make personal investments in their teams through coaching and long-term, genuine engagement with team members.

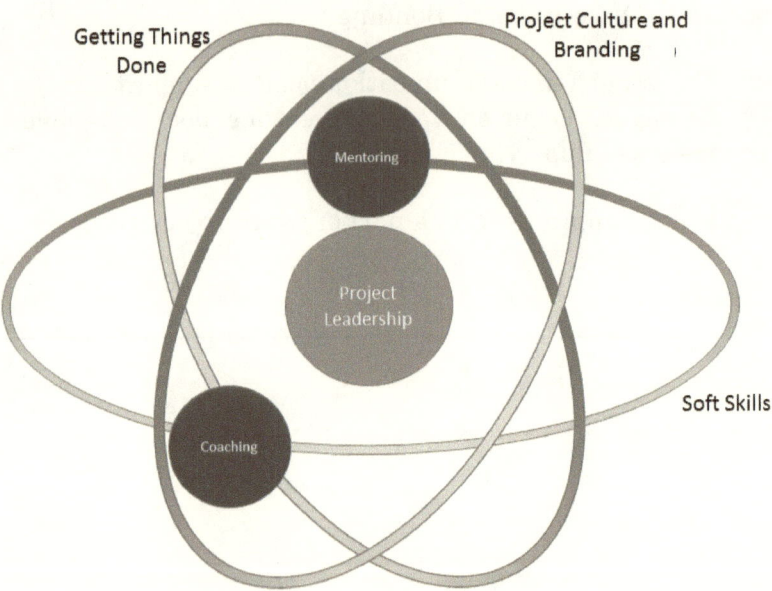

Building the Future

I believe that all the things about our jobs which we enjoy, we do for free. What we get paid for is all the crap we have to deal with.

Coaching is one of the things I do for free.

Why is coaching part of project leadership? After all, in many projects, there may be no expectation at all that you are coaching or training the people on your team. That may be organizationally out of scope, or you may have contractors on your team for whom you have no developmental responsibility.

There are several reasons to invest your time in coaching your team.

*   Coaching is investing in your project. While some of your coaching may be targeted on longer term development, much of it can build skills that will have a pay-off within the life of your project.

*   You are building for the future. This may be part of building your company's human assets. Even if it isn't, you are still building a network of colleagues along with your personal brand.

*   Coaching adds another layer to the connection of your team. They're not just doing a job, they're learning at the same time. Besides your coaching, they'll also develop a team culture of sharing information and ideas with each other.

*   Frankly, it feels good. You've learned a lot from your experiences and training, and it's great to be able to share that with others.

Coaching is more than just providing performance feedback. There are forms for that. Coaching is being engaged with your team and making a personal investment in their development.

Setting Expectations

When I took a supervisor skills class, I remember thinking: wow, if they'd told me what they were looking for, I would have been so much better at my job! The class taught me what a supervisor should look for, what they should provide feedback on, and so on. If only someone had told me what they were doing...

The first part of coaching is setting expectations.

People are more motivated by expectations and goals if they've set them themselves, so I like to ask my team members at the start of the project to sit down and think about a few questions before we meet.

*   How do they define personal success on the project?

*   How do they define the project's success?

*   What would be an absolutely tremendous, knock-your-socks off personal success?

*   What is something that they would like to learn on the project (even if it would appear out of scope for their role)?

To some, this exercise may seem as hokey as writing a professional statement. However, it's *the* first step in coaching.

First of all, people like talking about themselves. You may have to draw some people out on the subject, but that's what these questions help do. When they start talking about personal success, they're really talking about who they are. You'll learn a lot from that.

Next, if you can have an honest conversation with a team member about how they define success, you'll learn what they're values are. What do they care about? What motivates them? How they see themselves working with a team?

It should also become plain in the discussion how their personal success supports the project success. If nothing else, by asking someone to frame these together drives the mental connection of the two, and it shows that you consider both of them to be important.

I especially like to talk about what someone sees as a grand success. This is tremendously valuable in a situation where you are going to be providing performance feedback. They tell you what their stretch goal is. You talk about it, helping shape it to something achievable on the project. Then you've got it written down, ready to discuss at performance review time.

This is particularly important when you're working with people who are eager to prove themselves. Maybe they want to be promoted, maybe they just want the respect, or maybe they're angling for a good bonus. If the two of you can agree on what would be a fabulous success, they've got something concrete to work for, which is much easier than if they try to read your mind. You can also reflect back on this during the project, commending them for a success that matches this goal, or encouraging them to greater efforts.

Discussion of what else they'd like to learn is also enlightening. Maybe they'd like to expand their role, or just pick up some additional knowledge. Many times you'll hear simpler things, like, "I'd like to get more chances to do group presentations." If you know their interest, you can work with that. You'll have that enthusiasm to use if you need to decide who will work on a given task, or how to rearrange roles.

Again, just showing that genuine interest in someone else's development brings its own rewards.

That's all the first part of expectations: have team members establish their own.

However, you've got your own expectations to set. You can tell people what you're looking for, what you're expecting to see, and the quality of work you're expecting. You can tell people what else you think is important to project success.

This relates closely to topics in previous chapters about project risks. For example, in one case I expected communication with certain subject matter experts to be critical to the project. We needed them on our side, but not just superficially. We really needed to deliver for them. This meant constant communication and engagement. Even though this was out of the ordinary for the technical team members I had, I let them know that this was part of what we needed to do.

Some of your expectations can be very tactical and project-specific, such as frequency and style of communications, participation in a project cadence, issue escalation, and the like. Some of them can be more general or philosophical. Learning more about the business process, improving presentation skills, or learning a methodology or standard are examples of these.

With either category you are getting your teammate focused on the work to be done and how you think success will be achieved with it. Doing this at the start of the project, you are getting the team into the mindset to perform.

You should also share your own definition of project success, which is usually drawn from my own perception of the situation along with what has been shared with me by the project sponsor or stakeholders. I find that this sort of discussion not only informs my team about our objective, it coaches them on how others in the organization see the project.

Imagine you've got a project to build a website for a company. It's interesting work, maybe coming close to cutting edge technology, and the company is good to work for. Your team sees this and establishes an interest in the project work based on these factors.

Now imagine you know, as the project leader, that this website is considered strategically critical by the company. The company is banking its future on what your team delivers. Great rewards await project stakeholders if the project delivers, and, alas, penalties await if it fails.

To engaged team members, knowing this makes a difference. People enjoy being part of something big, but your team will also want to know that there's going to be pressure to deliver.

What Do You Coach About?

So far I've talked for several pages about coaching without ever making a direct statement about what you say when you're coaching. How do you coach? What do you coach? What do you coach *about*?

There are plenty of different models for coaching. What I've got here reflects the logical areas of coaching in a project context.

* Skill coaching - how to develop high-value, high-quality deliverables, how to establish a personal definition of done for a task, how to make effective use of one's skills in a project or company setting. This presumes that you do not need to directly instruct your team member on the rudiments of what they're doing, but that certainly may also take place.

* Coaching on professional behavior - how to improve interpersonal communication, development of presentation skills, development of verbal communications in formal and informal settings, interview skills. One would hope that this does not have to extend to basic social graces, but it may include coaching on what behavior is appropriate when meeting with a client or executive.

* Career coaching - how to understand the project and one's role to be ready for more responsibility on the next project. This can include how to handle ambiguity in a project situation, how to view project activities in a larger context, and what the next level of responsibility looks like. I also might explain why I made a certain decision, to satisfy the interest of a team member as well as to establish expectations for the future.

As an example of the latter, I had just joined a project in flight and I was in a meeting with a number of other people, discussing up-coming activities. I didn't know my team well yet, and was still coming to grips with the overall project objective. A question came to me: who would work on task X?

In a lot of cases, I would recommend deferring an answer when you don't have one. However, this was just a name to be put on a task list. "Dennis," I answered after giving it a moment's thought.

Afterwards, another team member asked me why I'd picked Dennis for the task. She said that she thought my answer showed that I didn't have any confidence in her, and she wanted to know why I was being unfair to her.

Our team members often think that every decision on a project is given thorough consideration with every factor being weighed. We all wish it could be so. In this case, I needed to make a decision with minimal information in five seconds, and I picked a team member I thought could do the task. I just needed a name!

I've known project executives who have come up with a well-worn bit of hogwash to explain their decision. I've known others who wouldn't have answered it at all. My answer was to explain that, in this case, there was no robust decision-making paradigm in use. I'd made a decision based on limited information and would have to handle the consequences if I was wrong. This was just part of being a project leader.

There was one another area of coaching that can arise: life coaching. I think of this as covering issues or concerns well beyond the project and a person's professional skills. Sometimes this may look a lot more like therapy than professional development, and when it does, you should take a good look at whether you're doing the right thing. You can easily go out of bounds with that, and you may not have the right background to be involved with that sort of discussion.

No matter what the nature of the coaching, keep in mind that the tone should be positive and constructive. Even when you may be suggesting that a task could be done better (or maybe has to be redone), you'll want to aspire to an educating and collaborative tone. That tone is a distinction of project leadership.

When Do You Coach?
Coaching, like many of the attributes of project leadership, is a habit, not a task.

It's a continuous activity, done in every action you perform and in every communication touch with your team members.

That said, there are also some practical guidelines. First and foremost, coaching should be a one-on-one activity. Much of the discussion may be private - even the positive comments - and this also means that it should not be publicly referred to after the fact.

Second, as discussed in the previous chapter on communication, show that it's important to you by scheduling time for these discussions. Keep a journal that you can refer to when you have a coaching session. I like to have these one-on-one discussions weekly with team members, knowing that they may blur project updates and issue resolution with your coaching. That's okay: just as you wouldn't walk into a networking event and declare, "I'm here for the networking", you want the coaching to consist of a natural discussion.

Third, expect to have impromptu sessions also. Maybe your team member will pull you aside to discuss a particular concern. Maybe you'll see a behavior that you want to respond to as soon as possible, not letting it go until your next scheduled session. You should work to keep these focused on the immediate issue, but let it expand if circumstances allow.

Is There a Difference Between Performance Feedback and Coaching?

You may be saying that coaching sounds a lot like feedback.

I think there are three critical differences between feedback and coaching.

First, coaching has a wider context. You're setting personal expectations, not based on the generic person filling a role or job title should be expected to deliver, but based on the team member's own aptitude and goals.

Second, coaching is directed over a wider span of time. While some of the coaching you'll provide has an immediate focus of attaining project objectives, you're also targeting long-term development. Performance feedback is only concerned about the behavior and delivery specific to the project.

Third, coaching is ultimately constructive. It is designed around building up your team member to take on more challenges and grow into them. Performance feedback may include constructive suggestions about actions to take in the future, but those will be primarily corrective in nature. They'll reflect what was done, or not done, on the recent project, and not project into the future.

What Is the Connection Between Coaching and Mentoring?

Much is made of mentoring in professional development. It is seen as the key to accessing career opportunities and getting focused and high-value professional coaching. Many people seek a "mentor", whom they may associate with superhuman powers which they hope they can contract through close association. Many companies try to establish mentoring programs to respond to this desire.

Coaching and mentoring would seem to have similarities, but they also have key differences.

Coaching and effective mentoring have similar goals of consciously developing a person's professional capabilities. However, coaching will tend to focus more on the immediate needs for the person's current project and the growth to follow. While a mentor might offer advice for a project situation, a mentor is not necessarily connected to the project and will more likely offer longer-term career-focused guidance.

An especially notable difference is that, as a project leader, you can take on the coaching role with the team members on your project. Effectively, you have been assigned to be a coach. Your common engagement on the project is enough to establish a coaching relationship with your team member.

Despite the attempts of many corporate mentoring programs, an assigned mentor rarely is effective. A mentoring relationship should be based on a developed connection between two people who mutually want to maintain the relationship. This is not easy to sustain when people have been essentially assigned to a relationship.

A coaching relationship can be tremendously productive, but it is ultimately limited by the lifespan of its project (unless it evolves into mentoring). The longer-term nature of mentoring and its deeper connection can make it even more meaningful, which is why so many people aspire to establish one.

It's Not You, It's Me

The activity and specifics of performance feedback are likely well-documented for your company. You will presumably have been trained to prepare and deliver such feedback, and this is so specific to your project's situation that there's no value in dwelling on it here.

There are times, though, where feedback can turn into a coaching situation.

On occasion I've joined a project and found myself warned about one of my new team members. They're not good communicators. They don't take criticism well. They don't follow through. (A parallel situation is having one of your team leads report that they have such a problem with a member of their team.)

Sometimes this critique is accurate, honest, and thorough. After all, there are poor performers out there.

I've also found that sometimes it's more reflective of the person providing the assessment. A common factor when I've seen this situation is that there was too little communication between the manager and the team member. It is often reflective of a personal disconnect (or dislike) between the two. In some cases, the manager set their (never-made-explicit) expectations thinking they had a more experienced person working with them, and therefore had less contact than the worker needed.

There's coaching needed here to re-establish the confidence of the person being evaluated. What can they do to make clear their own abilities? How can they re-establish their personal brand? How can they handle a similar situation going forward?

If appropriate, there's also a coaching opportunity for the person who made the assessment. What are they looking for? Did they make their expectations clear? If there were interpersonal issues, what could be done to resolve these, or at least keep them from impacting the project?

Performance feedback processes are usually very one-sided: we assume that the manager or supervisor is trained for this task, and is therefore providing an accurate and fair review. Since the bias of the person receiving a bad review is obvious, while the reviewer is theoretically unbiased, the process supports the reviewer completely.

As a project leader, it's important to remember that an evaluation is often a reflection of the interpersonal dynamic as much as one individual's personal contributions. There are two sides to the story, and for long-term coaching, it's worth learning more. An extremely negative evaluation can be a sign of an employee who should be counseled to seek opportunities elsewhere. It can also be a sign of a poor or disengaged manager.

Another situation where performance feedback can turn into coaching is where a project is not a complete success - it may even be a failure. A team member may feel that no matter what happened to the project, they personally met their objectives, showed personal development, and may have gone above and beyond in a way worthy of reward.

How do you deal with this situation?

This is a delicate question. On the one hand, it is hard to support rewards for a team member for personal accomplishment when the project team as a whole failed. It might seem needlessly cold to press a team member on what else they could have contributed that would have made the difference, but it might also be a legitimate question. On the other hand, we can conjecture any number scenarios where the relative lack of success of the project shouldn't be blamed on a specific team member. There could even be a case where nobody at all on the team should be blamed.

From a coaching perspective, you can try to filter through the experience to be as fair as possible. Some team members may indeed deserve positive feedback in this situation. Some team members might not. Providing feedback should always be a deliberate, thoughtful activity, but it should be especially so in this case.

You should also remind your team of what they've learned and what they've accomplished. You may have to remind yourself of that, too: as the project leader, you'll probably take the lack of success more to heart than anyone else.

I had this happen to myself. On a very technically challenging project, I worked harder and with a greater commitment than I'd ever worked before. I did everything I could think of to make the project successful, but to no avail. The project's success was marginal, at best. As the project leader, it doesn't seem right to claim that I did a good job when the project objectives weren't completely met. That is, if anyone's personal success should be connected to the project success, it should certainly have been mine.

From a self-appraisal point of view, I still struggle with the right answer for this. As a project leader, your team members deserve the same kind of struggle for the right answer.

A Case Study in Coaching

In one of my early projects as a project manager, I had a crash course in coaching, all with a single person. Perhaps because of that, it should be more of a cautionary tale than a true case study. Anyway, it illustrates some coaching challenges and how they can relate to performance and team operations.

The project was the same one I used as an example earlier in this chapter, and the person was the same one who had complained about not being assigned to a particular task. I'll call her Dee.

Again, I had joined the project in the middle of things. Even before I got there, my predecessor warned me that Dee was a project herself, although I didn't get any specifics.

Then, even while I was trying to establish my own tone for the project, which included the insistence that everyone could talk to everyone else, I had my own team members warning me that I shouldn't let Dee talk to the client. The specific issue noted was that she did not have a sense of appropriate communication in meetings. She couldn't adjust the level of detail she provided to match her audience, and she occasionally hijacked meetings to address her own questions.

I never actually saw this myself, however. I think this was merely a matter of luck (sometimes you do get lucky). Another problem came up first.

It turned out that Dee was hypoglycemic. To manage her blood sugar level, she needed to eat at very regular times. Unfortunately for her, there was no food in the building, not even a vending machine, and our team was working such crazy hours that project meal times were unpredictable, to say the least. Dee told me that she wanted to eat with the team, but

---

couldn't match our schedule and didn't feel like she should take time to eat with us if she'd already eaten. I counseled her to, first and foremost, take care of herself and eat when she needed to eat. Then she should join the team if she felt like it: her being part of the team was also important. While this falls into the life coaching category in the list above, I was able to address it in a limited way as professional behavior.

Around the same time, I uncovered what might have been the explanation for the pleas that I keep Dee from talking to anyone. She had issues with understanding voice tone and body language. This was two-way: she couldn't read someone else's tone or body language, but she was also not conscious of what messages she was sending herself. This was also life coaching, but something that needed to be addressed for the project. I coached her on reading body language and tone (and gave her a book on the subject), but couldn't do much more than that. Still, we were able to avoid any incidents in meetings, so I take that as a win, also.

Then we approached our conversion weekend. The conversion was planned for Saturday, but we anticipated follow-on work and support for Sunday. At any rate, we were working out of town and nobody was going home, so we were all going to be at the project site.

Dee approached me to explain that she observed Sunday as a day of quiet meditation and worship, and did not feel comfortable working on Sunday. Luckily I had a little time before having to answer that, so I canvassed people I knew for their input.

The suggestions were pretty much all the same: if she had completed her work, there should be no obligation to be at work on Sunday.

The problem was that there was no specific work assignment. This was a case where the work responsibility was simply being present.

My challenge was that, while I wanted to respect her beliefs, I also wanted to be fair to the rest of the team. Nobody *wanted* to be at the client on Sunday. In a situation like this, I didn't feel it was fair to say that one person's reason for not working was more valid than another's.

Finally I went back to discuss this with Dee. I explained my concern regarding the team and we discussed it. We eventually found a compromise where she would be away during the morning but then join the team for the afternoon. Perhaps not a perfect answer, but the team seemed satisfied and I hope that we all learned something about being part of a project team as a professional.

For the subjects mentioned (and others of smaller import), we had numerous coaching sessions adding up to many hours. Did I spend too much time with her? Most people would have decided she was too high maintenance well before working through some of my solutions, and it may have been that this was the point of the warnings I'd gotten when I joined the project.

In most circumstances, you won't have this much time to invest in a single person, and your team member should have been spending their time doing something more directly related to the objective. What's more, the project ended before we were able to see a pay-off from our collective investment of time. However, following up later, I learned that she had made marked improvements, been promoted, and was highly regarded. In the end, while this might not have been the best model of coaching (due to the extraordinary effort required), I still call that a success.

Chapter Wrap-up

Project leaders invest in their teams through coaching.

Coaching should be a planned, consistent activity and part of the project personality that you establish.

Performance feedback is a backward-looking assessment of performance, while coaching is a forward-looking communication to develop a team member's capabilities.

Mentoring is a long-term relationship focused on career growth and personal development.

Chapter 12: Project Leader to Project Believer

Many people, for a long time, have tried to make project management a repeatable, scientific activity. Standard project management artifacts and their supporting processes have been developed and iterated to achieve that goal. But as noted at the outset and implied by many of the examples in this book, even a scientific approach won't always get you what you want in the end.

Still, when we make a distinction between project management and project leadership, we extend the dream of predictable project success to project leadership. What can we do to make our successes repeatable?

I am reminded of the St. Louis Cardinals baseball team in the 1980s. They were a team built entirely on speed. The idea was that defense was better with fast players, and offense was better, too. They didn't have to be good hitters: they beat out ground balls because of their speed. They stole tons of bases. Their philosophy was that you can have a bad day at the plate, or a good day; a bad day pitching, or a good one; but speed always shows up at the ballpark.

Similarly, you may have team members with varying levels of skills, or an area where you just couldn't find someone who had the right skill at all. For yourself, you might have deep knowledge in certain business functions or technologies; if you rely on that knowledge to achieve success for your project, sometimes it will go well, but if you're asked to take on something outside of your strengths, it won't go as well.

By their definition, habit and character are there for you every day. Building project leadership on this foundation is a major step towards making project success a predictable, repeatable experience.

So what attributes of a project leader have we demonstrated?

A project leader:

* Has courage

* Has character

* Is vulnerable

* Easy to do business with

* Is genuine

* Focuses on delivering value

* Questions everything

* Mentally active

Let's recap.

A project leader *has the courage* to ask tough questions and propose radical solutions to project problems.

A project leader demonstrates *character* and trust in all their relationships, working for the betterment of the team and the achievement of the project's objectives.

A project leader is *vulnerable*, asking others for help, conferring with team members and others on decisions, and deferring to others as appropriate.

A project leader is *easy to do business with*, finding positive ways and constructive ways to work with team members, project stakeholders, and subject matter experts.[7]

A project leader is *genuine*, speaking sincerely, demonstrating respect, and being honest and fair.

A project leader *focuses on delivering value*, sharing ownership of project outcomes with project stakeholders and working to achieve project success, not just project completion.

A project leader *questions everything*, making sure that every aspect of a project is the best answer for the project, not simply the default standard.

A project leader is *mentally active*, anticipating problems and collaborating with team members to find creative solutions to issues.

---

[7] Thanks to *Reengineering the Corporation*, 1993, by Michael M. Hammer.

Project Leader to Project Believer

A common thread throughout this is that project leadership is a positive exercise; it is focused on positive, constructive actions, not negative, destructive ones. While projects take talent, logic, and sound management skills to achieve success, they also require belief. They require belief in the objective, belief in the team, and belief that the team can achieve the objective. The project leader has to become the first project believer, leading the rest of the team to share in that belief. With that power in force, the team can approach every problem with the belief that it can be solved.

Back a million years ago I was doing consultant boot camp. One of the exercises we did was supposed to be about negotiating skills. In it, our group split into pairs. In each pair, participant A represented a company that wanted to buy a certain stock of apples for use in their manufacturing process. Participant B represented a company that wanted to buy the same apples for their own peculiar needs. Implied conflict: it's a zero-sum game, and only one of us can have these apples.

However, in each case, the participants quickly amicable resolved a situation whereby the apples were shared between the two companies. It turned out that the two companies needed different parts of the apple, so it wasn't a zero-sum game after all. Now, I have no idea if you could really put apples through multiple manufacturing processes and not just get apple sauce out of it, but that wasn't the point. The point was that the negotiations were cheerful and successful because *every single one of us went into the exercise assuming there was a solution.*

Imagine that. Imagine your next interaction with a crazy teammate, incompetent boss, or slacker intern. You could go into it expecting to be disappointed, that excuses would be made, randomness would ensue, and nothing would get done. Or you could believe that things would turn out well, and a mutually beneficial arrangement could be made. Okay - let's be realistic. It won't always turn out well. But if you don't look for the win-win, you're never going to find it.

That's project leadership. That's being a project believer.

www.ingramcontent.com/pod-product-compliance
Lightning Source LLC
Chambersburg PA
CBHW031944170526
45157CB00002B/385